Investigating with Relational GeoSolids™

By

Karen Lindebrekke

Dana C. Hupert

ETA Cuisenaire

Vernon Hills, Illinois

A Special Thank You!
A special thank you to Maria Knuth for her contribution to this book.
Maria wrote early drafts of the student pages for some of the activities.
We greatly appreciate her input and support.

Math Product Development Manager: Bill Gasper
Editors: Barbara Brandt, Terri Pope-Hellmund, Brion McGinn
Cover Design: John Pocius
Text Design and Production: ETA/Cuisenaire Creative Services Department

Investigating with Relational GeoSolids™

ISBN 1-5716-22136
ETA 9311

ETA/Cuisenaire • Vernon Hills, IL 60061-1862
800-445-5985 • www.etacuisenaire.com

Printed in United States of America.

09 10 11 12 13   13 12 11

Contents

Overview

Investigating with Relational GeoSolids™ offers hands-on mathematical investigations for students in grades 6–10. The activities in this book focus on using a scientific approach coupled with concrete models called Relational GeoSolids, to demonstrate and explain complex mathematical ideas.

Relational GeoSolids are ideal for teaching such topics as naming and classifying figures, attributes of solids, nets for solids, relationships among lines and planes, cross-sections of solids, patterns, metric and customary measurement, surface area, volume, density, and affecting surface area and volume by altering dimensions.

There are 14 solids in a Relational GeoSolids set. There are two sets of dimensions for each solid—the exterior and interior dimensions. The approximate interior dimensions are given for each solid. The exterior dimensions are all $1/8$" larger than these approximations (2.125" or 1.125"). Descriptions of the geometric solids included in the set follow.

The **sphere** has a diameter of approximately two inches.

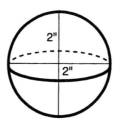

The **hemisphere** is half the size of the sphere above. Thus, the volume of the hemisphere is about half that of the sphere.

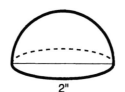

There are two **cylinders** with the same heights, but different diameters. Each cylinder has an altitude of approximately 2 inches, but the diameter of the larger cylinder is approximately 2 inches, and the diameter of the smaller cylinder is approximately 1 inch. The volume of the large cylinder is about four times that of the small cylinder.

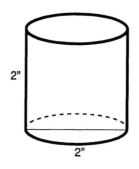

The **cone** has an altitude of approximately 2 inches and a diameter of approximately 2 inches. The volume of the cone is about one-third that of the large cylinder.

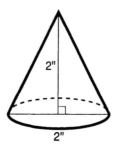

There are two pyramids—a **triangular pyramid** and a **square pyramid**. Each pyramid has an altitude of approximately 2 inches, and the lengths of the sides of the bases are also each about 2 inches. Note that the base of the triangular prism is not congruent to the triangular faces of the pyramid. The volume of the triangular pyramid is about one-third that of the large triangular prism, and the volume of the square pyramid is about one-third that of the large cube.

There are two **triangular prisms** with the same height, but different-sized bases. Each triangular prism has an altitude of approximately 2 inches. The sides of the base of the large prism are approximately 2 inches; however, the sides of the base of the small prism are approximately 1 inch. The volume of the large prism is about four times that of the small prism.

There are four rectangular prisms: a **large cube,** a **small cube,** a **square prism,** and a **rectangular prism**. The sides of the large cube are each approximately 2 inches; the sides of the small cube are each approximately 1 inch. The altitude of the square prism is approximately 2 inches, and the sides of the base are each approximately 1 inch. The dimensions of the rectangular prism are 2 inches by 2 inches by 1 inch. Thus, the volume of the square prism is about twice that of the small cube, the volume of the rectangular prism is about twice that of the square prism, and the volume of the large cube is about twice that of the rectangular prism.

The **hexagonal prism** has an altitude of approximately 2 inches and a base approximately 2 inches across. The sides of the base are approximately 1 inch each. The volume of the hexagonal prism is about six times that of the small triangular prism.

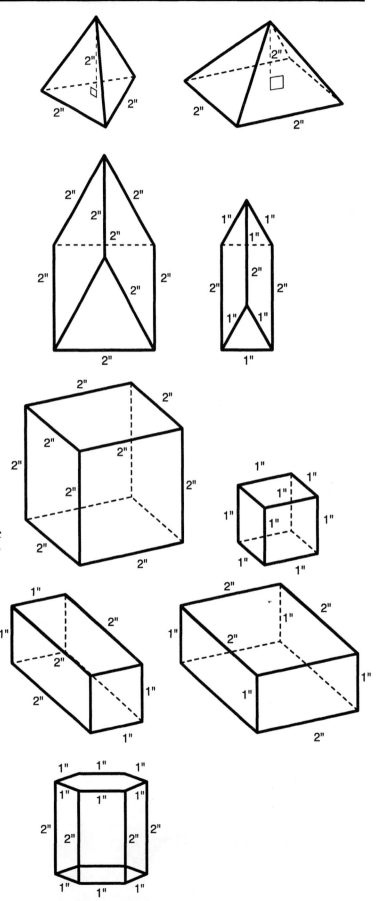

Manipulatives at the Secondary Level?

Primary and elementary teachers recognize that hands-on activities with manipulatives allow students to take a more active role in learning mathematics. With manipulatives, students are better able to visualize concepts and develop insights.

With such a laudable reputation, it seems unusual that manipulatives are used less frequently in middle school and high school. No research exists which indicates that manipulatives stop being effective after the elementary grades. Why, then, do teachers omit manipulatives in the presentation of difficult, abstract concepts?

Some middle school teachers might say that students at this age are more difficult to manage, more easily distracted. Physical objects, like manipulatives, are often noisy and add to the disruption. For these reasons, teachers at this level often present material in a way that ensures a quieter environment—the teacher speaks, and the students listen. But, as studies have indicated, traditional methods do not promote better understanding or retention. Quality learning of mathematics should involve the visual and kinesthetic learning styles as well as analytical thinking that hands-on activities with manipulatives promote.

Relational GeoSolids offer students the opportunity to discover for themselves many of the concepts and relationships associated with geometric solids. They can use the solids to make nets to determine surface area, and they can fill them with various substances to determine volume and density. Instead of just applying given formulas and memorizing concepts presented in a textbook, students will discover and verify such formulas and concepts by collecting and analyzing data.

While many of your students may have used manipulatives in earlier grades, it is essential that you clearly outline your expectations of how students should use the manipulatives during each activity. These might include guidelines about appropriate use and care of the equipment, as well as distribution, inventory, and cleanup procedures. In addition, you might consider using cafeteria trays to confine any spills that may occur.

After students make their predictions in each activity, you might want to allow time for them to experiment appropriately with the shapes. However, the best experimentation will occur if you first provide some direction and connection to the upcoming activity, as suggested in the *Getting Started* sections in the teacher pages.

A teacher's mastery of the manipulative is vital to a lesson's success. Be certain to work the selected activity with the appropriate manipulatives several times before presenting the lesson to students. It is important that you not only anticipate student questions, but that you also are able to offer suggestions and guidance. The more confident you appear to your students, the more willing they will be to take risks and to experiment.

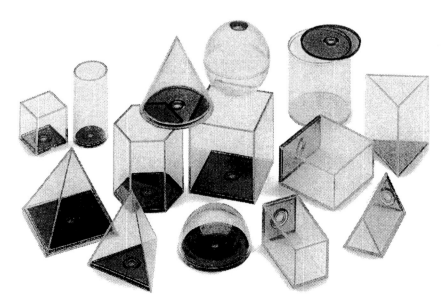

Meeting the NCTM Standards

Relational GeoSolids and the activities in this book support the National Council of Teachers of Mathematics (NCTM) *Curriculum and Evaluation Standards*.

Mathematics as Problem Solving The activities in this book promote problem solving. Specifically, in each activity, students are presented with a question. They predict the solution to the question based on their observations and prior knowledge. Then they test their predictions by experimenting with the Relational GeoSolids.

Mathematics as Communication Students work in pairs and share their hypotheses, observations, and conclusions with each other. They must also explain their thinking in writing.

Mathematics as Reasoning Students analyze their results; then, based on their discussions, they draw conclusions and make generalizations. They also must justify their thinking in writing.

Mathematics as Connection Students make connections to the real world. In particular, the activities in this book demonstrate the strong connection between math and science.

Topics Chart

Relational GeoSolids sets, when used with the activities in this book, are ideal for teaching and/or reinforcing the following mathematics topics.

Math Topics	Investigations													
	1	2	3	4	5	6	7	8	9	10	11	12	13	14
Naming and classifying figures	x	x												
Attributes of solids	x	x					x							
Nets for solids			x	x	x									
Relationships among lines and planes				x										
Cross-sections of solids						x								
Patterns							x							
Customary measurements					x				x	x	x	x	x	x
Metric measurements									x	x	x			
Surface area					x								x	x
Volume								x	x	x	x	x	x	x
Density												x		
Ratios														x
Percents											x			
How changing dimensions affects surface area					x								x	x
How changing dimensions affects volume								x	x				x	x

How to Use this Book

The 14 hands-on investigations in this book can replace and/or supplement your textbook curriculum. Activities are organized according to mathematical topic, and to some extent, in a developmental way. You can, however, use them in any order, depending on your curriculum plans and students' previous experiences. Each investigation can be completed in one or two 45-minute class sessions.

To determine how the activities fit into your curriculum, refer to the Table of Contents on page 1 and the Topics Chart on page 5.

Each activity consists of six pages; the first four are designed for students, the next two for teachers. These contain suggestions for getting started, procedural ideas, and answer keys. In preparation for class, make a photocopy of the student pages for each student and carefully review the teacher pages. Some of the *Getting Started* suggestions involve the use of other materials.

Teacher pages are organized as follows:

Objectives Clearly states those skills and behaviors that students should be able to demonstrate at the end of the activity.

Getting Started Provides pre-teaching ideas and suggestions for how and when to introduce the activity.

Procedure Provides sample responses for Results Charts where students test their predictions and record discoveries made through experimentation.

Mathematical Review Presents some preliminary background information and suggests methods for introducing students to the mathematics involved in the activity.

Predict the Results Provides students with an opportunity to predict the outcome of the investigation before they get started. This gives you an opportunity to assess students' knowledge of the topic as they begin to investigate.

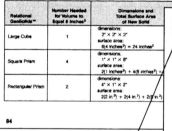

Discussion Questions Provides sample responses to thought-provoking questions that help students analyze their results and draw conclusions.

Further Investigations Provides sample solutions to more challenging opportunities that apply acquired skills from the lesson, often to real-world situations.

Assessment Opportunities

As a teacher using Relational GeoSolids, you observe your students daily, listen to their discussions, look carefully at their work, and use this information to guide your teaching. While it is important for you to monitor student thinking and understanding, students should also be encouraged to reflect on their own progress. Each investigation contains a *Discussion Questions* section which evaluates students' understanding of the concepts learned in the activity. These questions give students an opportunity to share their results with other students. This section also contains thought-provoking questions to help you assess students' understanding of the concepts presented in the activity.

- An Assessment Chart on page 93 is provided to help you follow and record student progress. At the top of the Assessment Chart, a four-point scoring rubric will help you analyze what students have learned, and determine how well they have progressed from concrete to symbolic understanding.

- Encourage students to reflect on their work at the culmination of each investigation by asking themselves questions such as—

  ▶ What did I learn by doing this investigation?

  ▶ What did I find difficult/easy about this investigation?

  ▶ What did I do well in completing this investigation?

  ▶ What did I like best/least about this investigation?

  ▶ What ideas introduced in this investigation still confuse me?

Additional Sources of Information

The following additional resources are available from ETA/Cuisenaire®. To order, refer to the ETA product number that is provided in bold-faced type.

Assessment Standards for School Mathematics. National Council of Teachers of Mathematics. **ETA 4165**

Curriculum and Evaluation Standards for School Mathematics. National Council of Teachers of Mathematics. **ETA 4144**

Professional Standards for Teaching Mathematics. National Council of Teachers of Mathematics. **ETA 4145**

Hands-On Geometry. Scott Purdy. **ETA 909**

Additional Materials

- Nets for Relational GeoSolids™ **ETA 4169**
- ManipuLite® Base Ten Components—Units (1 cm³) **ETA 321**
- Dry Filler Material (Plastic Rice) **ETA 9471**
- Liter Pitcher **ETA T8-563QA**
- Graduated Measuring Cylinders **ETA 6210**
- Precision School Balance **ETA 410B**
- Additional Gram Weight Set **ETA 418**
- Sorting Sets:
  Ceramic Tiles **ETA 476**
  Rocks and Pebbles **ETA 478**
  Shells **ETA 481**
  Hardware—Screws and Bolts **ETA 482**
  Nuts and Washers **ETA 477**

Investigation 1: What's in a Name?

A formal name should contain enough information not only to clearly identify an object or organism, but also to differentiate it from others that may be similar. Names, therefore, usually have more than one part, such as *Swiss cheese*.

That's easy . . . letters! Now do I get some cheese?

The scientific names of organisms also consist of two basic parts: the genus and the species. For example, *Mus musculus*, is a common house mouse. Other types of mice are *Peromyscus maniculatus*, a deer mouse, and *Peromyscus leucopus*, a white-footed mouse. Organisms with the same genus name are more closely related than those with different genus names. Therefore, a deer mouse and a white-footed mouse are more closely related to each other than they are to a house mouse.

In a similar way, many geometric solids have names with more than one part. By comparing their names, you can determine how they are related.

Topic of Investigation

- *Names of geometric solids*
- *Relationships among similarly named solids*

Questions to Investigate

- ▶ *What is a* **prism**?
- ▶ *What is a* **pyramid**?
- ▶ *How are geometric solids named?*
- ▶ *What can you tell from the name of a geometric solid?*
- ▶ *Why is it important to accurately name an object or organism?*

Mathematical Review

Compare the names of these geometric solids.

Octagonal Prism   Triangular Prism

The names tell us that these solids are similar because they are both prisms, but also that their bases have different shapes. Most solids are named according to the shape of their bases.

Some mathematical terms you need to know:

Base – for simplicity, let the base of each Relational GeoSolid™ figure be represented by its green, or bottom, face. (Bear in mind, however, that in some types of solids the top face is also considered to be a base.)

Face – a planar (flat) surface of a geometric solid.

Polygon – a closed, plane (2-dimensional) figure with three or more sides.

© ETA/Cuisenaire®

Investigating with Relational GeoSolids™

Predict the Results

Look at the names of the geometric solids in Results Chart 1. Without looking at the solids or drawings of them, predict the total number of each of the following for one Relational GeoSolids set.

Predictions Chart: Total Number of Each Type of Face

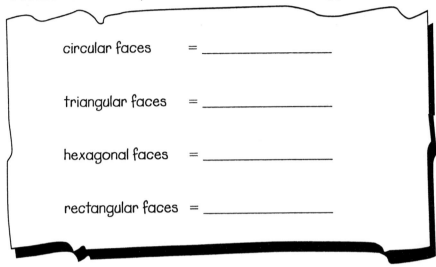

circular faces = _____

triangular faces = _____

hexagonal faces = _____

rectangular faces = _____

Procedure

1. Examine each of the geometric solids listed in the chart and determine the following:

    a. the shape of the base

    b. the shape of the top

    c. the shape and number of other faces

    Record your answers in Results Chart 1.

2. Using the data in Results Chart 1, determine the total number of each of the following:

    a. circular faces

    b. triangular faces

    c. hexagonal faces

    d. rectangular faces

    Record these totals in Results Chart 2.

Materials

For each pair of students:

▶ *1 Relational GeoSolids set*

Results Chart 1: Characteristics of Geometric Solids

Relational GeoSolids™ Shape	Shape of Base	Shape of Top	Shape and Number of Other Faces
Large Cube			
Small Cube			
Square Prism			
Rectangular Prism			
Large Triangular Prism			
Small Triangular Prism			
Hexagonal Prism			
Large Cylinder			
Small Cylinder			
Triangular Pyramid			
Square Pyramid			
Cone			
Sphere			
Hemisphere			

Results Chart 2: Total Number of Each Type of Face

Shape of Face	Total Number in Set
Circle	
Triangle	
Hexagon	
Rectangle	

Investigating with Relational GeoSolids™

Discussion Questions

1. Compare your predictions with your results.

    a. Do they match? If not, how are they different?

    b. Explain why your predictions differ from the results.

2. Look at the results for the prisms.

    a. What type of shape makes up the base of a prism?

    b. What can you conclude about the base and top of each prism?

    c. What conclusion can you make about the shape and number of the other faces that make up each prism?

    d. Write a definition for *prism*.

3. Look at the results for the cubes. Cubes are special types of rectangular prisms.

    a. Explain why a cube is a rectangular prism.

    b. How do cubes differ from other rectangular prisms?

4. Look at the results for the cylinders. Cylinders are not prisms.

    a. Explain how cylinders are similar to prisms.

    b. Explain how cylinders differ from prisms.

    c. Read your answer to problem #2d. Is your definition specific enough to exclude cylinders? If so, explain how it excludes cylinders. If not, write a revised definition.

5. Look at the results for the pyramids.

    a. What type of shape makes up the base of a pyramid?

    b. What conclusion can you make about the shape and number of the other faces that make up each pyramid?

    c. Write a definition for *pyramid*. Be sure to exclude cones, just as you excluded cylinders from the definition for prisms.

Further Investigations

1. Describe the shape and number of each type of face in a decagonal pyramid.

2. Describe the shape and number of each type of face in a decagonal prism.

3. The prisms and cylinders in this Relational GeoSolids set can be more accurately described by adding the term *right* to the name, such as *right triangular prism* and *right cylinder*. What does the term *right* tell you about these solids? Draw a cylinder that is not right.

Objectives

- Recognize how geometric solids are named.
- State the definition and basic attributes of a prism.
- State the definition and basic attributes of a pyramid.
- Deduce the basic characteristics of geometric solids from their names.
- Explain why it is important to accurately name an object or organism.

Getting Started Lead students in a discussion about why people have more than one name. One reason is that it provides a means of recycling favorite first names (useful in a world with more than six billion people). Unrelated people can usually be told apart by their last names. Similarly, first names and middle names help differentiate among people with the same last name. Thus,

assigning more than one name to a person provides a means of identifying individuals by name while also indicating whether they are likely to be related through blood, marriage, cultural, or regional ties. Discuss with students how the genus and species method of naming organisms achieves a similar goal. Then, explain that a similar system is used for naming geometric solids.

Mathematical Review As necessary, go over the Mathematical Review material with students. Instead of providing a formal definition for the term *base*, which requires students to understand the term *altitude*, students are simply told to consider the green face of each solid as its base. After students have written their predictions, remind them that a *square* is a type of rectangle.

Predict the Results Remind students to make thoughtful predictions and not to change them as they work.

Procedure

1. Circulate among students to ensure that they understand the task. Remind them that for this activity the term *base* refers only to the green face, although in later activities the top face of a prism will also be referred to as a base.

2. Encourage students to check their answers in Results Chart 1 before completing Results Chart 2, since any errors they make in the first chart will negatively affect their answers in the second chart.

Results Chart 1: Characteristics of Geometric Solids

Relational GeoSolids™ Shape	Shape of Base	Shape of Top	Shape and Number of other Faces
Large Cube	rectangle or square	rectangle or square	4 rectangles or squares
Small Cube	rectangle or square	rectangle or square	4 rectangles or squares
Square Prism	rectangle or square	rectangle or square	4 rectangles
Rectangular Prism	rectangle	rectangle	2 rectangles, 2 squares
Large Triangular Prism	triangle	triangle	3 rectangles
Small Triangular Prism	triangle	triangle	3 rectangles
Hexagonal Prism	hexagon	hexagon	6 rectangles
Large Cylinder	circle	circle	none
Small Cylinder	circle	circle	none
Triangular Pyramid	triangle	point or none	3 triangles
Square Pyramid	rectangle	point or none	4 triangles
Cone	circle	point or none	none
Sphere	none	dome or none	none
Hemisphere	circle	dome or none	none

Results Chart 2: Total Number of each Type of Face

Shape of Face	Total Number in Set
Circle	6
Triangle	12
Hexagon	2
Rectangle	37

Discussion Questions

1a. Predictions and answers will vary. Students should, however, address whether their predictions match their results and how they are different.

1b. Answers will vary. For example, a student may indicate he forgot that squares are types of rectangles, so he predicted that there would be only 21 rectangular faces, instead of 36.

2a. A polygon makes up the base of a prism.

2b. The base and top of a prism are the same size and shape (they are congruent).

2c. All the other faces of a prism are rectangles, and the number of side faces equals the number of sides of the base.

2d. A prism is a solid figure with a polygon for a base and a congruent polygon for the top. All of the sides are rectangles, and the number of side faces equals the number of sides of the base.

3a. A cube is a rectangular prism because squares are rectangles, so it has a rectangle for a base, a congruent rectangle for the top, and all other faces are rectangles.

3b. In cubes, all of the rectangles are squares.

4a. In a cylinder, as in a prism, the base and top are congruent.

4b. In a cylinder, there are no rectangular faces, and the bases are not polygons.

4c. Yes, my definition works, because it says that the base of a prism must be a polygon, and circles are not polygons.

5a. A polygon makes up the base of a pyramid.

5b. All other faces of a pyramid are triangles, and the number of side faces equals the number of sides of the base.

5c. A pyramid is a solid figure with a polygon for a base and a point at the top. All of the sides are triangles, and the number of side faces equals the number of sides of the base.

Further Investigations

1. A decagonal pyramid contains 1 decagon and 10 triangles.

2. A decagonal prism contains 2 decagons and 10 rectangles.

3. Right means perpendicular, so the sides of a right prism or cylinder are at a 90° angle to the base. A cylinder that is not right might look like this:

Investigation 2: How Do You Make a Key?

Most people think a *key* is a tool that is used to unlock something. However, there is another type of key, one that is used to sort or classify objects and organisms. When using or creating this type of key, step by step you are "unlocking" the identity of the object or organism. Keys can be created as flowcharts or as lists of statements and/or questions about the object. Usually these statements either apply or do not apply to the object or organism, and the questions can be answered with a simple *yes* or *no*. Such a key is called a *dichotomous key*. Dichotomous literally means "cut in two," since there are two outcomes for each statement or question.

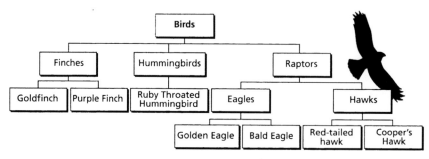

Topic of Investigation

Classification of shapes according to their characteristics

Dichotomous keys

Questions to Investigate

▶ *How can you make a classification key?*

▶ *How can geometric solids be sorted and classified?*

▶ *What characteristics define different kinds of geometric solids?*

Mathematical Review

Prism a three-dimensional figure whose top and bottom faces are congruent polygons in parallel planes. Both the top and the bottom faces are actually both referred to as a **base**. The side or **lateral** faces of prisms are all rectangular.

Pyramid a three-dimensional figure with a single **base** in the shape of a polygon and lateral faces that are all triangular. These triangular faces all meet at a single point (or **vertex**) called an **apex**, located opposite the base.

As shown below, prisms and pyramids are named according to the shapes of their bases.

Triangular pyramid

Hexagonal prism

In this Investigation, you will make a classification key to use for sorting and naming the three-dimensional objects in your Relational GeoSolids set according to their characteristics.

Investigating with Relational GeoSolids™

Predict the Results

Study the "My Pets" classification key shown at the bottom of this page. Then, without looking at the actual solids or the classification key on the following page, consider the similarities and differences among the various geometric solids in your set. Think about the different characteristics you might use to distinguish one group of solids from the others, and how you could organize these categories to make a classification key. Write your predictions in the chart below.

Predictions Chart: Characteristics Used in a Relational GeoSolids Classification Key

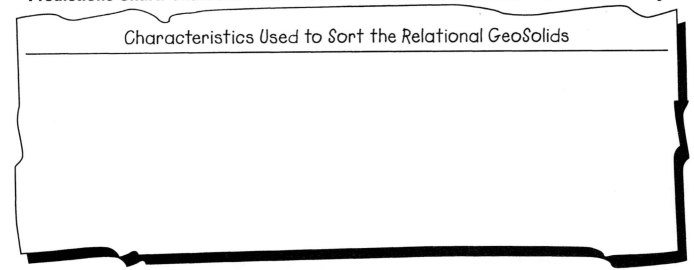

Characteristics Used to Sort the Relational GeoSolids

Procedure

1. Examine the dichotomous classification key on the following page and attempt to determine where each of the geometric solids should go. Trace downward, eliminating solids until only one remains. Once you determine that solid, enter the name in the corresponding blank.

2. For the remaining blanks, fill in the characteristic which best fits. You will want to look at the other branch of the key to see what this division excludes. You will also want to look at the solids which fit into this branch in order to determine the appropriate characteristic.

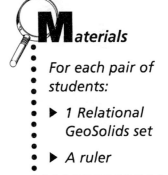

Materials

For each pair of students:

▶ *1 Relational GeoSolids set*

▶ *A ruler*

A Sample Classification Key

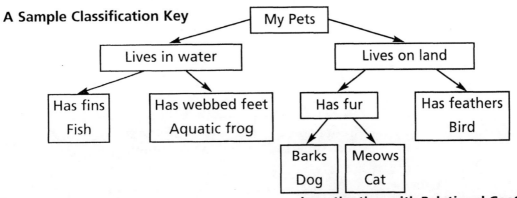

Results Chart: Geometric Solids Classification Key

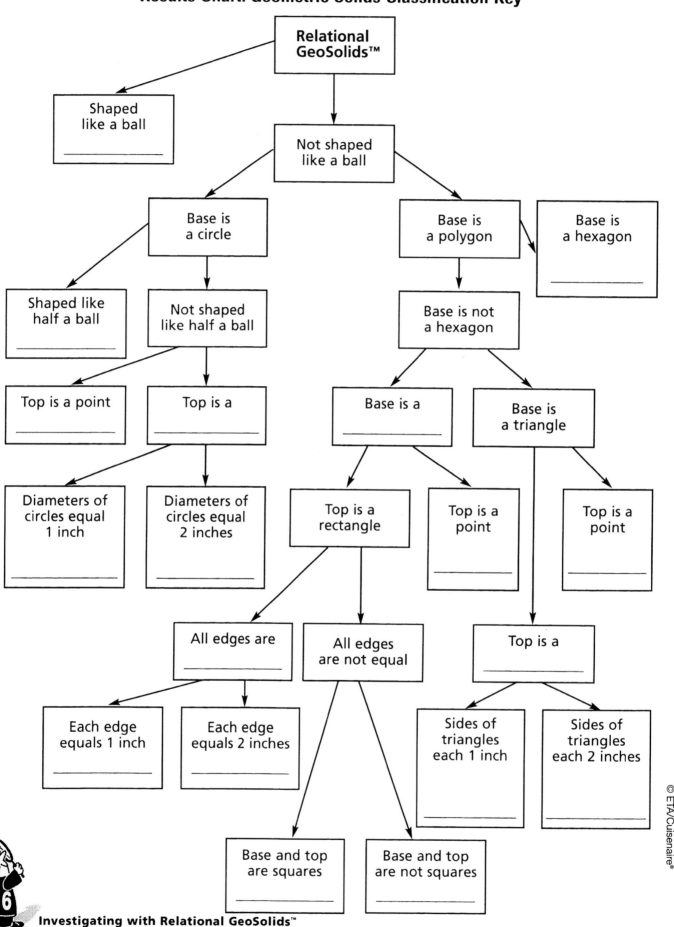

Investigating with Relational GeoSolids™

Discussion Questions

1. Compare your predictions with the characteristics used in the flowchart.

    a. Do your predictions match your results? If not, how are they different?

    b. Explain why your predictions differ from your results.

2. Using just the prisms (small cube, large cube, hexagonal prism, rectangular prism, square prism, small triangular prism, and large triangular prism), create another key using a different sorting method.

3. **a.** How many divisions did the original chart contain? (In other words, how many times did you have to split up groups in order to single out every solid?)

    b. How many branches did your smaller chart contain?

    c. Can either of these be improved upon? Why or why not?

    d. How many divisions would a set of 25 items need to separate out every item?

4. Study the following key for a small set of geometric solids.

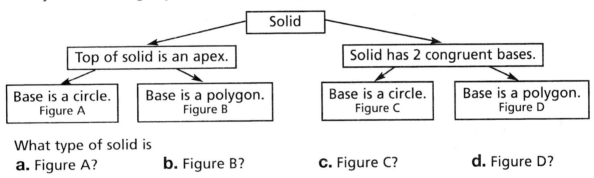

    What type of solid is
    a. Figure A?   **b.** Figure B?   **c.** Figure C?   **d.** Figure D?

Further Investigations

1. Design a flowchart-style dichotomous key for some other group of objects or organisms, such as pine, oak, or maple trees (classify these trees by the characteristics of their needles or leaves).

2. Design a different form of a dichotomous key for the Relational GeoSolids or for some other objects, which uses GOTO statements like those in computer programs. The sample key below is for common U.S. coins.

    1a. This coin is silver colored . . . . GOTO 2

    1b. This coin is copper or brown colored . . . . Penny

    2a. The edge of this coin is serrated (ridged) . . . . . . GOTO 3

    2b. The edge of this coin is smooth . . . . Nickel

    3a. The diameter of this coin is between 2–3 cm . . . Quarter

    3b. The diameter of this coin is less than 2 cm . . . . Dime

Investigating with Relational GeoSolids™

Objectives

- Sort and classify solids according to their characteristics.

- Design and construct a dichotomous key for classifying solids.

Getting Started Ask students how scientists decide how to group different animals and plants. Explain to students that, in general, animals, plants, and objects are grouped according to their shared characteristics. For example, birds have feathers and lay eggs, whereas mammals have fur or hair and nurse their young, who are born live. There are many ways to present such information: Venn diagrams, flowcharts, or plain text. In this activity, students will fill in gaps in a flowchart that serves as a classification key.

Consider making a key with the class for sorting a group of objects, such as students' shoes. Have each student give you one shoe. Discuss how the shoes could be sorted into two major groups. One way to sort them is whether they have laces or not. Continue sequentially sorting the shoes into two groups, constructing a flowchart on the board as you work with the class. Have students retrieve their shoes as they are singled out in the key.

Mathematical Review Go over the review on the student pages. Be sure that students understand each of the terms.

Predict the Results Remind students to make thoughtful predictions and not to change their predictions as they work.

Procedure

See the Results Chart on the following page. Circulate among students to ensure that they understand the task and are correctly filling in the *dichotomous* keys. Make sure they realize that a branch terminates only when it comes to a single solid.

Discussion Questions

1a. Predictions and answers will vary. Students should, however, address whether their predictions match their results and how they are different.

1b. Answers will vary. For example, a student may indicate that her predictions differ from the key because she hadn't considered all the different characteristics of the solids.

2. Answers will vary, but students should create a new chart that varies significantly from the original key. Make sure that the keys sort according to an attribute, not by name. A sample key is provided below.

3a. Students should count 13 divisions, although they may come up with 26 branches.

3b. Students should create charts with 6 divisions.

3c. As long as students did create charts with only 6 divisions, neither chart can be reduced. It requires one fewer division than the number of objects to create a chart, because each division can separate out a different object.

3d. Since it requires one less division than the given number of objects, the total number of divisions needed would be 24.

4a. Figure A is a cone.

4b. Figure B is a pyramid.

4c. Figure C is a cylinder.

4d. Figure D is a prism.

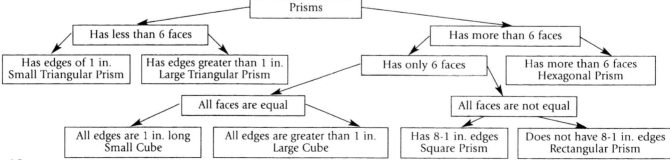

Results Chart:
Geometric Solids Classification Key

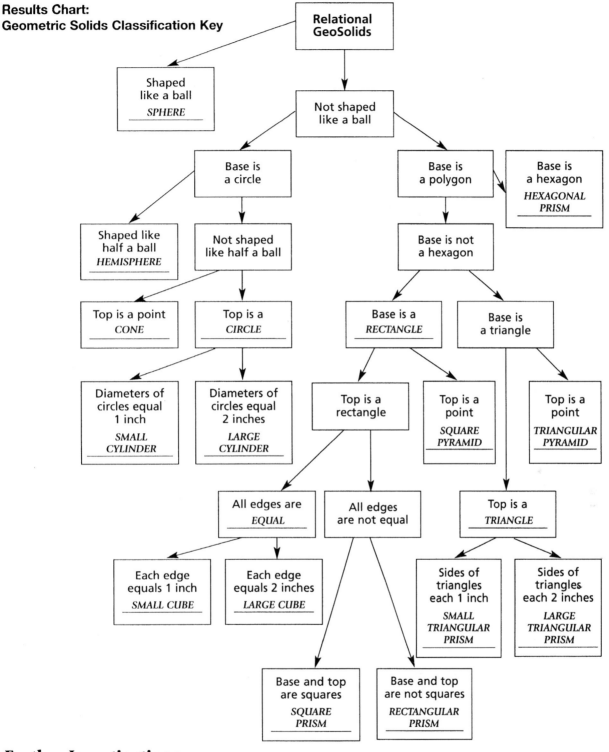

Further Investigations

1. Keys will vary based on the objects or organisms classified and the students' approaches. Check each student's key by using it to sort the objects yourself, or have students use and critique each other's keys. If students design keys for trees or other organisms, they may use field guides as references.

2. Go over the sample key for U.S. coins with students to ensure that they understand how to use the GOTO key. Student keys will vary depending upon the approaches they take and the objects sorted if they are given choices or different assignments.

Geometric solids are three-dimensional shapes that can be created by folding two-dimensional patterns called **nets**. A manufacturer may use nets to make products such as boxes. An engineer or architect may use nets to make scale models of large structures. In this activity, you will explore and create a variety of nets for the Relational GeoSolids.

"What do you mean, *without* a net?"

Topic
of Investigation

Nets that form various geometric solids

Questions
to Investigate

▶ *Which solids will have nets that appear similar?*

▶ *How many nets can be used to create a specific solid?*

▶ *How does the number of sides on a solid affect its net?*

▶ *What does the net of a solid represent?*

Mathematical Review

The **net** of a solid is a two-dimensional representation that can be folded to create a three-dimensional solid. Each face of the solid is represented by a shape in the net. Each line or fold in the net represents an edge of the solid.

Two possible nets for a cube are shown below. Only the figure on the left, though, is an actual net because it could be folded along each line to form a cube, whereas the figure on the right could not. Although the figure on the right looks similar to the one on the left and has the correct number of squares to form the faces of the cube, the squares are not in the right places.

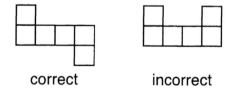

correct   incorrect

It may be difficult to visualize what is and what is not a net, so you will use modeling clay or poster board to create nets for the various solids. You will discover that many solids have more than one possible net.

Investigating with Relational GeoSolids™

Predict the Results

Look at a list of names of Relational GeoSolids. Without looking at the actual solids or drawings of them, answer the following questions:

a. Which solid's nets will be most similar to the nets of the rectangular prism? Explain.

_____

_____

b. Which solid's nets will be most similar to the nets of the square pyramid? Explain.

_____

_____

Procedure

1. Use modeling clay or poster board to create three different nets each for these solids: the large cube, large triangular prism, rectangular prism, square pyramid, and triangular pyramid.

    a. Roll out the modeling clay to about a one-fourth inch layer. Press one face of the solid in the clay, then pivot it along its edges to press each of the other faces in the clay. To make a net from poster board, pivot the solid the same way, tracing around each face of the solid with a pencil.

    b. Cut out and fold your net to make sure that it forms the intended solid.

    c. Sketch a smaller model of the net in the space provided in the Results Chart. For the triangular pyramid, label or shade the base in your sketches.

2. To make a net for the cylinder, first use a water-based marker to draw a vertical line on the side of the solid. Place the cylinder so the line is touching the edge of the clay closest to you. Roll the cylinder away from you for one complete revolution until the line on the cylinder is in the same position on the clay as when you started. The distance between the beginning and ending positions of the line represents the circumference of the cylinder.

Materials

For each pair of students:

▶ *1 Relational GeoSolids set*

▶ *1 container of modeling clay or 1 full-size poster board*

▶ *Scissors, a pencil, a water based marker, and masking tape*

▶ *A metric or customary ruler*

▶ *1 set of Nets for Relational GeoSolids*

3. Make a net for a cone the same way. Be sure to include the bases of the cylinder and the cone in your nets. Use a similar method to make the nets out of poster board.

4. Create two different nets each for the cylinder and the cone, and sketch each net in the space provided in the Results Chart.

5. Compare your nets for a cube with those created by other students. How many different nets for a cube did your class find? Record your answer in the space provided below the Results Chart.

Results Chart: Sketches of Nets for Relational GeoSolids

Geometric Solid	Sketches of Nets		
Large Cube			
Large Triangular Prism			
Rectangular Prism			
Square Pyramid			
Triangular Pyramid			
Large Cylinder			
Cone			

How many nets did your class find? _____

Investigating with Relational GeoSolids™

Discussion Questions

1. Compare your predictions with your results.

   a. Do they match? If not, how are they different?

   b. Explain why your predictions differ from the results.

2. Compare the different nets you created for each Relational GeoSolid.

   a. Is the amount of material required to make each different net for a given geometric solid the same?

   b. Will this always be true? Why is this the case?

   c. About how much material was required to make the net for the large cube? Explain.

   d. What mathematical measure is represented by the amount of material required to make a net?

3. Examine the perimeters of the different nets you drew for the geometric solids.

   a. Is the number of exposed edges on the nets for a certain Relational GeoSolid always the same? Justify your answer.

   b. Are all the perimeters of the nets for a certain Relational GeoSolid always the same? Justify your answer.

4. Examine the sketches of the different nets you drew for the geometric solids. For which solids did you draw all the possible nets?

Further Investigations

1. You have found several different nets for a cube. How many more are there? Find all the possible nets for a cube.

2. Sketch at least 6 different nets for a regular hexagonal prism. Are there others? Why are there so many nets for this solid?

3. Draw or describe the basic structure of a net for a soccer ball.

4. Geologists encounter several of the solid shapes above in mineral crystals, plus many solid shapes that are much more complicated. Research one of the other solid shapes exhibited by crystals, such as a rhombohedron, a hexagonal bipyramid, an octahedron, or a rhombic dodecahedron. Describe and build a model of the crystal structure by making a net; then name at least one mineral that exhibits this crystal structure.

23

Investigating with Relational GeoSolids™

Objectives

- Define the term *net* and create different nets for various solid figures.

- Define the relationship between a solid's net and its surface area.

Getting Started Ask students whether they know what a net for a solid is. If so, draw the two figures shown in the mathematical review on the board. Ask students which one is an actual net for a cube. If you are using Nets for Relational GeoSolids, you may want to demonstrate and/or have students explore how the cross-shaped net folds around the cube. Have students explain why the other figure is not a net. If students do not know what a net is, have them read over the Mathematical Review.

Next, have students draw a different net for a cube. Be sure they understand that a different net is not merely a *transformation* (rotation or reflection) of another net. Also, explain that the shapes (faces) that make up a net should not connect just at the corners; they should connect along the edges, except for cones and cylinders because this is not an option for these two shapes. Explain to students that they will be exploring the different nets that can be constructed for each Relational GeoSolid.

Mathematical Review As necessary, go over the review provided on the student pages. Be sure that students understand highlighted terms.

Predict the Results Remind students to make thoughtful predictions and not to change their predictions as they work.

Procedure

1. Demonstrate how to use the modeling clay or poster board to make the cross-shaped net for a cube. If you and/or the students have a set of Nets for the Relational GeoSolids, allow students to explore how each net wraps around its respective solid. Students may then sketch the nets as their first entries in the Results Chart for each solid. (If you do not allow them to include these nets in their Results Charts, adjust the answer key to the Results Chart

   and Discussion Question 4. Students will be able to find only two nets for the triangular pyramid.) Point out that the base of the triangular pyramid is not congruent to the faces of the pyramid. Have students shade or label the base of the triangular pyramid in their sketches of its nets.

2. Ask how many possible nets there are for cylinders and cones. (Theoretically, there are infinitely many nets for these solids.)

Results Chart: Sketches of Nets for Relational GeoSolids

Geometric Solid	Sketches of Nets		
Large cube			
Large triangular prism			
Rectangular prism			
Square pyramid			
Triangular pyramid (consider having students label or shade the base)			
Large cylinder			
Cone			

Discussion Questions

1a. Predictions and answers will vary. Students should, however, address whether their predictions match their results and how they are different.

1b. Answers will vary. For example, students may say that they thought the triangular pyramid and the square prism would have similar nets, but they didn't consider the big differences in the numbers of triangles and rectangles in the nets. Or, they may have thought there would be only six nets for a cube, since it only has six faces.

2a. Yes, the amount of material required to make each net for a given solid will always be the same.

2b. This will always be true, because the amount of material needed to make a net is the same as the amount of material needed to make the solid, which is fixed for a given solid.

2c. The length of a side of the large cube is approximately 2 inches, so, each face is about 4 inches^2. There are 6 faces. 6×4 inches$^2 = 24$ inches^2.

2d. The amount of material needed to make a net is equal to the surface area of the solid.

3a. Yes, the number of exposed edges on the nets for a given solid appears to be the same. This is true for all the nets drawn for each solid.

3b. No, unless all edges of the solid are congruent, as in a cube, there is no guarantee that the perimeters of the nets will be the same. The pyramids show this because the triangular faces are not equilateral, so different nets can have different perimeters. (Students may have different justifications based on the nets they drew.)

4. All of the nets were found only for the triangular pyramid because there are only 3 possible nets. (Students may also indicate they found all the nets for a cube, which they were instructed to do in the Procedure Section.)

Further Investigations

1. Encourage students who have not already done so to persevere until they have determined the 11 possible nets for a cube.

2. Student answers will vary because of the vast number of nets for this solid. One possible set of nets is:

There are a large number of nets for this solid because it has so many edges. (Accept other reasonable explanations.)

3. A soccer ball's net is made from pentagons and hexagons—each pentagon is surrounded by 5 hexagons.

4. Student reports will vary, based on the mineral crystal or the solid shape they chose to research.

Sample answers for two of the examples provided on the student pages follow.

octahedron a cube with the corners cut off, or two square pyramids placed base to base.
Net: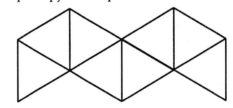

Minerals that exhibit this crystal structure include diamond, gold, magnetite, and silver.

rhombohedron a form whose sides are made up of 6 rhombi.
Net: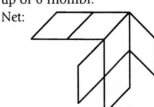

Minerals that exhibit this crystal structure include dolomite, cinnabar, and smithsonite.

Investigation 4: How Do Lines and Planes Relate?

Representations of both lines and geometric planes can be found everywhere we look. Understanding how lines and planes relate interests professionals in many different fields. For example, pilots and air traffic controllers need to determine whether two aircraft are likely to cross paths, and, if so, how to avoid such an incident. Other professionals that need to understand these relationships are artists, architects, astronomers, engineers, geologists, and oceanographers. In this activity, you will learn about the various relationships between lines and planes, and where you might observe them in everyday life.

"Flight 4080, you're cleared for takeoff."

Topic
of Investigation

Parallel, intersecting, and skew lines

Parallel and intersecting planes

Questions
to Investigate

▶ *What do parallel and intersecting lines look like?*

▶ *What do parallel and intersecting planes look like?*

▶ *What are skew lines?*

▶ *How are lines and planes related to geometric solids?*

Mathematical Review

A **line** is an infinite number of points that has no thickness. It extends in two opposite directions and never ends. A line is named with two points, such as line *AB*. If two lines lie in the same plane, they are either parallel or they intersect.

Intersecting lines cross at exactly one point.

Parallel lines never intersect.

Skew lines are neither parallel nor intersecting, because they lie in different planes. The concept of skew lines is probably not as familiar to you as parallel and intersecting lines, but you can see examples of skew lines almost anywhere you look. In a room, for example, the vertical line formed by two intersecting walls and the horizontal line formed between a third wall and the ceiling are skew lines. These do not intersect, and, since one is vertical and the other horizontal, they cannot be parallel.

A **plane** is a surface that extends infinitely, but has no thickness. Planes are named with three points, such as plane *ABC*.

Parallel planes do not intersect each other.

Intersecting planes form a line. Any two planes are either parallel or intersecting.

Investigating with Relational GeoSolids™

Predict the Results

In this activity, the edges of the geometric solids will model lines and the faces of solids will model planes. Without looking at either the solids or at the drawings of the solids, try to predict whether the prisms and pyramids found in your set of Relational GeoSolids™ will model the figures listed in the chart. Write *YES* or *NO* in each column of the chart. *Remember:* Consider only the lines modeled by the edges; do not consider the infinitely many lines that actually exist in a plane.

Predictions Chart: Types of Lines and Planes Modeled by Relational GeoSolids

Figure	Will All <u>Prisms</u> in the Set of Relational GeoSolids Model These Figures?	Will All <u>Pyramids</u> in the Set of Relational GeoSolids Model These Figures?
Parallel Lines		
Intersecting Lines		
Skew Lines		
Parallel Planes		
Intersecting Planes		

Procedure

1. Examine each of the solids shown in the Results Chart. Determine whether the edges and faces of each solid model parallel, intersecting, and/or skew lines and parallel and/or intersecting planes.

2. If the solid contains the lines or planes listed in the chart, give at least one example of each. Remember that lines are named with two points, such as line *AB*, and planes are labeled with three points, such as plane *ABC*. Write *NONE* if there are no examples of the types of lines or planes listed for a solid.

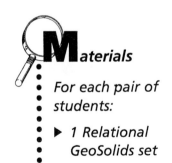

Materials

For each pair of students:

▶ *1 Relational GeoSolids set*

27

Results Chart: Types of Lines and Planes Modeled by Relational GeoSolids

Relational GeoSolids Shape	Parallel Lines	Intersecting Lines	Skew Lines	Parallel Planes	Intersecting Planes
Triangular Prism					
Hexagonal Prism					
Triangular Pyramid					
Square Pyramid					
Cube					

Investigating with Relational GeoSolids™

Discussion Questions

1. Compare your predictions with your results.

    a. Do they match? If not, how are they different?

    b. Explain why your predictions differ from the results.

2. In this activity, faces modeled planes and edges modeled lines.

    a. How does a face of a solid differ from an actual plane?

    b. How does an edge of a solid differ from an actual line?

3. Look at the hexagonal prism shown in the Results Chart.

    a. How many edges of the solid are parallel to the plane *GJK*? Name the edges.

    b. How many sides of the solid are parallel to line *AB*? Name the faces.

    c. How many edges of the solid are parallel to line *AB*? Name the edges.

4. **a.** An airplane is flying due north at an altitude of 25,000 feet. Another airplane flying due west at an altitude of 30,000 feet passes directly overhead. What type of lines do the flight paths of these two airplanes represent?

    b. An airplane is flying due east at an altitude of 21,000 feet. Another airplane flying due west at an altitude of 28,000 feet passes directly overhead. What type of lines do the flight paths of these two airplanes represent?

5. In your classroom, find examples of the following types of lines and planes. List one example for each:

Parallel lines: Parallel planes:

Intersecting lines: Intersecting planes:

Skew lines:

Further Investigations

1. When a plane intersects another plane, a line is formed. What is the relationship between the two lines formed when a plane intersects two parallel planes? Try to find an example of this in your classroom and draw a sketch of it.

2. Geologists examine the orientations of the planes in which different layers of rocks lie and the relationships among the planes. They define the orientation of a rock slab's surface (geologic surface) in space by its *dip* and *strike*. Rocks often have several *partings* (separations), however, and actually have several surfaces (planes) with different orientations in space. The orientation of a line formed from the intersection of two such planes is described using *trend* and *plunge*. Research these terms: *dip*, *strike*, *trend*, and *plunge*. Explain how these measures are used to help determine fault lines, geological history, and the probability of future landslides.

Objectives

- Describe the different relationships that exist between lines and planes, using mathematical language.

- Identify examples of the different relationships between lines and planes modeled by the edges and faces of Relational GeoSolids™.

Getting Started Ask students to define a *line* and a *plane* and to give examples from objects in the classroom. Next, go over the Mathematical Review with the class. Have students use pieces of paper to represent planes and pencils to represent lines. Remind them that, in actuality, lines and planes extend infinitely. Ask students to use their pencils and paper to model a line intersecting a plane, and two intersecting planes. (Students may want to cut slots in their paper to make them intersect.) Then ask them to model two parallel planes, two parallel lines, and a line parallel to a plane.

Finally, ask them to use their pencils to model a pair of skew lines. Ask whether two planes or a plane and a line could be skew. Explain why they cannot be. Tell students that they will investigate the different relationships between lines and planes by using various Relational GeoSolids as models, with the edges modeling lines and the faces modeling planes. Remind students of the definitions of *edges* and *faces*.

Mathematical Review Go over the review provided on the student pages. Have students model the different relationships described previously. Be sure they understand each of the terms.

Predict the Results Remind students to make thoughtful predictions and not to change them as they work.

Procedure

1. Circulate among students to ensure that they understand the definitions and can apply them to the task.

2. Make sure that students use two points to name the edges (lines) and three points to name the faces (planes). Sample answers are given below.

Results Chart: Types of Lines and Planes Modeled by Relational GeoSolids™

Relational GeoSolids™ Shape	Parallel Lines	Intersecting Lines	Skew Lines	Parallel Planes	Intersecting Planes
Triangular prism	AC and DF	AB and BC	AC and EF	ABC and DEF	ABC and BCF
Hexagonal prism	AB and GH	AB and BC	AB and GL	ABG and DEK	ABC and ABG
Triangular pyramid	NONE	AB and BC	AB and CD	NONE	ABC and ABD
Square pyramid	AB and CD	AB and BC	AB and DE	NONE	ABC and ADE
Cube	AB and CD	AB and BC	AB and FG	ABC and EFG	ABC and ADE

Discussion Questions

1a. Predictions and answers will vary. Students should, however, address whether their predictions match their results and how they are different.

1b. Answers will vary. For example, a student might indicate that she did not really understand skew lines until she worked with the Relational GeoSolids, so several of her predictions for skew lines were incorrect.

2a. A face differs from an actual plane because a face has boundaries (edges), whereas a plane extends infinitely in all directions. A face also has thickness, whereas a plane does not.

2b. An edge differs from a line because an edge is really a line segment (it has endpoints). Also, it could be considered to have thickness because the faces that form the edge have thickness, whereas a line or line segment has no thickness.

3a. Six edges are parallel to plane *GJK*: *AF*, *FE*, *DE*, *CD*, *BC*, and *AB*.

3b. Two faces are parallel to line *AB*: *DEKJ* and *GHIJKL*.

3c. Three edges are parallel to line *AB*: *DE*, *JK*, and *GH*.

4a. The flight paths represent skew lines.

4b. The flight paths represent parallel lines.

5. Answers will vary. Sample answers follow:

Parallel lines—the front edge of the ceiling and the front edge of the floor

Intersecting lines—a side edge of the floor and the front edge of the floor

Skew lines—the front edge of the ceiling and a side edge of the floor

Parallel planes—the front wall and the back wall

Intersecting planes—the front wall and a side wall

Further Investigations

1. The two lines formed from the intersection of a plane and two parallel planes are also parallel. A classroom example is the intersection of a back wall with the ceiling and floor. The edges formed at the top and bottom of the back wall are parallel.

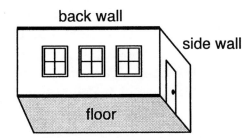

Floors and ceilings make parallel lines when they intersect a wall.

2. The *strike* of a geologic surface is the compass direction of the line of intersection between the inclined, geologic surface and the horizontal plane. The *dip* of a geologic surface is the acute angle formed by the intersection of the inclined, geologic surface and the horizontal plane.

When the planes of two geologic surfaces intersect, they form a line. The compass direction of this line is called the *trend*, and the angle of incline from the horizontal plane is called the *plunge*.

The lines formed where the planes of geologic surfaces intersect are *fault lines*. These lines tell geologists about the history and future stability of the rocks. The trend and plunge of the fault lines give information about the location and nature of possible landslides.

Investigation 5: How Do You Find the Surface Area of a Solid?

A solid's surface area can be found by totaling up the areas of each face or surface of the solid. If you were to construct a cube, the surface area of the cube would be equal to the total area of the paper used. People in many different professions—engineers, scientists, architects, and building contractors, for example—often need to determine the surface areas of solids. In this activity, you will determine the surface area of various geometric solids, and investigate how changing the dimensions of a solid affects its surface area.

Topic of Investigation

Surface area formulas for solids

Questions to Investigate

▶ How do the number and shape of the faces on a solid relate to its surface area?

▶ How can you calculate the surface area of a solid that has rounded surfaces?

▶ How does changing the dimensions of a solid affect its surface area?

Mathematical Review

Surface area refers to the area of the outer surfaces that make up the solid.

Lateral surface area of a solid only includes the faces or surfaces that make up the sides of the solid, not its base(s).

Total surface area is the sum of the areas of *all* its faces, including its base(s); that is, its lateral surface area plus the area of its base(s). In developing your methods for finding the surface areas of various Relational GeoSolids, look for shortcuts to avoid having to individually calculate the area of each face in a solid.

A net of a solid is a two-dimensional pattern that can be folded to create that three-dimensional solid. Since the net is made up of all the faces of the solid, you can use nets to help you develop your surface area formulas.

Ratios tell how two or more values compare, expressing the comparison in lowest terms. Fractions are one way of expressing ratios, but they may also be expressed with a colon. If your class contains 15 girls and 10 boys, there are 3 girls for every 2 boys. The ratio of the number of girls to the number of boys is written as 3:2 and is read as "3 girls to 2 boys."

Predict the Results

Look at the list of geometric solids below. Without looking at the actual solids or drawings of them, predict the various shapes that each of the solids will model. For the purposes of the investigation, it will be helpful to distinguish between squares and rectangles.

Predictions Chart: Shapes Needed to Determine Surface Area

Relational GeoSolids Shape	Shapes Modeled by the Faces
Cube	
Square Prism	
Triangular Prism	
Triangular Pyramid	
Square Pyramid	
Cylinder	

Procedure

1. If nets for the solids are provided, proceed to step 2. Otherwise, use modeling clay or poster board to create one net for each the solids listed in the chart above. Create the nets as follows:

    a. To make a net out of poster board, pivot the solid along its edges and trace around each face of the solid with a pencil.

    To make a net for the cylinder, use a water-based marker to draw a vertical line on the side of the solid. Roll the cylinder away from you tracing one complete revolution. The distance between the beginning and ending position of the line represents the circumference of the cylinder.

    b. Cut out and fold the nets to make sure they actually form the intended solids.

2. Look at your net for the solid. Determine the shapes for which you will need to find the area to determine the total surface area of the solid. Record your answers in Results Chart 1.

3. Next, list the area formulas needed for the different shapes in Results Chart 1. Be sure to tell what dimension each variable represents.

Materials

For each pair of students:

▶ *1 Relational GeoSolids set*

▶ *A full-sized sheet of poster board, a pencil, and scissors; or 1 set of Nets for Relational GeoSolids*

▶ *A customary ruler*

4. In Results Chart 2, write either formulas for, or explanations of, calculating the lateral and total surface areas of the solid. Remember, lateral surface area does not include the base(s). Use the same variables you used in Results Chart 1.

5. Repeat steps 1–4 for each geometric solid listed in the chart.

Results Chart 1: Formulas Needed to Find the Areas of Faces (Surfaces)

Relational GeoSolids Shape	Shapes Modeled by the Faces	Formula Needed for Each Shape
Cube		
Square Prism		
Triangular Prism		
Triangular Pyramid		
Square Pyramid		
Cylinder		

Results Chart 2: Formulas/Explanations for Calculating the Surface Areas of Solids

Relational GeoSolids Shape		Formula or Explanation
Cube	Lateral Surface Area	
	Total Surface Area	
Square Prism	Lateral Surface Area	
	Total Surface Area	
Triangular Prism	Lateral Surface Area	
	Total Surface Area	
Triangular Pyramid	Lateral Surface Area	
	Total Surface Area	
Square Pyramid	Lateral Surface Area	
	Total Surface Area	
Cylinder	Lateral Surface Area	
	Total Surface Area	

Investigating with Relational GeoSolids™

Discussion Questions

1. Compare your predictions with your results.

    a. Do they match? If not, how are they different?

    b. Explain why your predictions differ from your results.

2. Measure one side each of the small and large cubes to the nearest inch.

    a. What is the ratio of the lengths of their sides (large cube:small cube)?

    b. Determine the surface area of each cube. Show your work.

    c. What is the ratio of their surface areas (large cube:small cube)?

    d. How does doubling the dimensions of a cube affect its surface area? Explain why this happens.

3. Measure the diameter and height of the small cylinder to the nearest inch.

    a. Determine the surface area of the small cylinder. (You may report your answer in terms of π.)

    b. Which would increase surface area more: doubling the diameter or the height of the small cylinder? (You may report your answer in terms of π.) Show your work.

    c. Why does the surface area not increase by the same amount when either the radius or the height of the small cylinder is doubled?

4. The formula for the surface area of a sphere is $4\pi r^2$ where r represents the radius of the sphere.

    a. Calculate the surface area of a sphere with a 1-inch radius and a sphere with a 3-inch radius. (Report your answers in terms of π, as it will make question 4b easier.)

    b. What is the ratio of their surface areas (large sphere:small sphere)?

    c. How does tripling the radius of a sphere affect its surface area? Explain why this happens.

Further Investigations

1. Use a net for the cone to determine its lateral and total surface areas. Show all your work and explain your methods. (You may report your answers in terms of π.)

2. Increasing the amount of exposed surface area on an object increases the rate at which various reactions occur. Suppose a 4-inch cube of iron ore were broken into eight 2-inch cubes. Determine the total surface area of the iron ore when it is whole versus when it is broken into eight pieces. In which case would the iron ore oxidize (react with oxygen to produce rust) faster—when it is whole or when broken apart?

Objectives

- Develop formulas for finding the surface areas of various solids.

- Explore how changing the dimensions of a solid affects its surface area.

Getting Started Bring in an orange and a soup can with a label. Ask students what mathematical measure the orange peel represents, if they ignore its thickness. Explain that it represents the surface area of the orange. Then ask students what mathematical measure is represented by the soup can label, if they ignore overlap. Explain that it represents the lateral surface area of the can. Next, ask students how they could find the total surface area of the can. Explain that they would need to find the area of either the top or the bottom of the can, double it, then add it to the lateral surface area. This would give them the total surface area. Tell students that they will investigate ways to determine the lateral and total surface areas of various solids. They should look for shortcuts like that suggested for finding the total surface area of the soup can—i.e., doubling the area of one lid, because the two lids are congruent.

Mathematical Review As necessary, go over the review provided on the student pages. Be sure that students understand each of the terms.

Predict the Results Remind students to make thoughtful predictions and not to change their predictions as they work.

Procedure

1. If students are provided with Nets for Relational GeoSolids, they may go on to Step 2. If not, demonstrate how to make a poster board net for a solid. They may use either the large or the small versions of the cube, triangular prism, and cylinder to make their nets.

2. Encourage students to use their rulers to see whether the triangular base is congruent to the other faces in the triangular pyramid.

3. Remind students to use variables consistently for the dimensions of the solid. Consider introducing students to the terms *altitude* and *slant height* and their respective variables, a and ℓ, so that they can use these variables in their formulas.

4. Remind students to first find the formula for lateral surface area then total surface area, which includes the base(s).

Results Chart 1: Formulas Needed to Find the Areas of Faces (Surfaces)

Relational GeoSolids™ Shape	Shape and Minimum Number Needed of Each	Formula Needed for Each Shape
Cube	1 square	s^2, where s = length of side
Square prism	1 square, 1 rectangle	s^2 and $s \times h$, where s = length of side of base, h = height
Triangular prism	1 triangle, 1 rectangle	$\frac{1}{2} \times s \times a$, $s \times h$, where s = length of side of base, a = altitude of base triangle, h = height of prism
Triangular pyramid	2 triangles	$\frac{1}{2} \times s \times a, \frac{1}{2} \times s \times \ell$, where s = length of side of base, a = altitude of base triangle, ℓ = slant height
Square pyramid	1 square, 1 triangle	$s^2, \frac{1}{2} \times s \times \ell$, where s = length of side of base, ℓ = slant height
Cylinder	1 circle, 1 rectangle	$\pi \times r^2$, $2 \times \pi \times r \times h$, where r = radius, h = height of cylinder

Results Chart 2: Formulas/Explanations for Calculating the Surface Areas of Solids

Relational GeoSolids™ Shape		Formula or Explanation
Cube	Lateral Surface Area	$4 \times s^2$, where s = length of side
	Total Surface Area	$6 \times s^2$
Square prism	Lateral Surface Area	$4 \times s \times h$, where s = length of side of base, h = height
	Total Surface Area	$(2 \times s^2) + (4 \times h \times s)$
Triangular prism	Lateral Surface Area	$3 \times s \times h$, where s = length of side of base, h = height of prism
	Total Surface Area	$(3 \times s \times h) + (s \times a)$, where a = altitude of triangle
Triangular pyramid	Lateral Surface Area	$\frac{3}{2} \times s \times \ell$, where s = length of side of base, ℓ = slant height
	Total Surface Area	$(\frac{1}{2} \times s \times a) + (\frac{3}{2} \times s \times l)$, where a = altitude of triangle at base
Square pyramid	Lateral Surface Area	$2 \times s \times \ell$, where s = length of side of base, ℓ = slant height
	Total Surface Area	$s^2 + (2 \times s \times \ell)$
Cylinder	Lateral Surface Area	$2 \times \pi \times r \times h$, where r = radius, h = height
	Total Surface Area	$(2 \times \pi \times r^2) + (2 \times \pi \times r \times h)$

Discussion Questions

1a. Predictions and answers will vary. However, students should address whether their predictions match their results and how they are different.

1b. Answers will vary. For example, a student may indicate that she didn't realize that all the triangles in the triangular pyramid are not congruent.

2a. The ratio is 2:1.

2b. The large cube's surface area = $6 \times (2 \text{ in.})^2 = 24 \text{ in.}^2$
The small cube's surface area = $6 \times (1 \text{ in.})^2 = 6 \text{ in.}^2$

2c. The ratio is 4:1.

2d. Doubling the dimensions of a cube increases the surface area by a factor of 4, because the factor of increase is squared by the formula for surface area.

3a. The surface area of the small cylinder is $(2 \times \pi \times (0.5 \text{ in.})^2) + (2 \times \pi \times 0.5 \text{ in.} \times 2 \text{ in.}) = 2.5\pi \text{ in.}^2$ ($= 7.85 \text{ in.}^2$).

3b. Doubling the radius of the small cylinder increases the surface area more than doubling its height. Doubling the radius: $(2 \times \pi \times (1 \text{ in.})^2) + (2 \times \pi \times 1 \text{ in.} \times 2 \text{ in.}) = 6\pi \text{ in.}^2$ ($= 18.84 \text{ in.}^2$). Doubling the height: $(2 \times \pi \times (0.5 \text{ in.})^2) + (2 \times \pi \times 0.5 \text{ in.} \times 4 \text{ in.}) = 4.5\pi$ ($= 14.13 \text{ in.}^2$).

3c. Doubling the radius increases the surface area more because the radius is a factor in both terms and it is squared in one of the terms.

4a. The surface area of a sphere with a radius of 3 inches = $4 \times \pi \times (3 \text{ in.})^2 = 36\pi \text{ in.}^2$ ($=113.04 \text{ in.}^2$).
The surface area of a sphere with a radius of 1 inch = $4 \times \pi \times (1 \text{ in.})^2 = 4\pi \text{ in.}^2$ ($=12.56 \text{ in.}^2$).

4b. The ratio is 9:1.

4c. Tripling the radius of a sphere increases the surface area by a factor of 9, because the factor of increase is squared by the formula for surface area.

Further Investigations

1. The lateral surface area for the cone is a part of a circle: $(164°/360°) \times \pi \times (2.5 \text{ in.})^2 = 2.85\pi \text{ in.}^2$ ($= 8.95 \text{ in.}^2$). Then add the area of the circular base to find total surface area: $2.85\pi \text{ in.}^2 + (\pi \times (2.25 \text{ in.})^2) = 7.91\pi \text{ in.}^2$ ($= 24.8 \text{ in.}^2$).

2. The iron ore would oxidize faster when it is broken apart, because there is more surface area. The surface area of a 4-inch cube = $6 \times (4 \text{ in.})^2 = 96 \text{ in.}^2$. The surface area of eight 2-inch cubes = $8 \times 6 \times (2 \text{ in.})^2 = 192 \text{ in.}^2$.

Investigation 6 : What Shapes Can You Make by Intersecting Planes with Solids?

Scientists and engineers need to determine the shapes that are formed when three-dimensional objects are intersected by planes. The result of such an intersection is referred to as a *cross section*. Often the area of these cross sections must be determined. For example, a geologist might need to predict the area of rock that would be exposed if it were to fracture along a certain plane. Or, a physicist or biologist may need to determine the cross-sectional area of a pipe or blood vessel to determine how much liquid will flow through it at a given velocity.

Mathematical Review

A plane is a surface that extends infinitely but has no thickness. Planes can be oriented in infinitely many ways. Planes can be modeled by flat surfaces such as walls, tabletops, or pieces of paper; remember, however, that planes really have no edges, because they extend indefinitely. Thus, models of planes are really just pieces of planes.

When a plane intersects a three-dimensional solid figure, it divides the solid into two parts. The plane creates a flat surface on each part of the solid where it cut through. Flat surfaces are two-dimensional shapes—rectangles, circles, triangles, etc. For example, the intersection of the horizontal plane with the cylinder below is a circle.

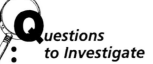

Topic of Investigation

Shapes formed by intersecting planes with solids

Questions to Investigate

▶ *How many different ways can a plane intersect a given solid?*

▶ *How does the shape of a solid determine the possible shapes that can be formed when a plane intersects it?*

▶ *What shape(s) can always be formed when a plane intersects a prism?*

▶ *What shape(s) can always be formed when a plane intersects a pyramid?*

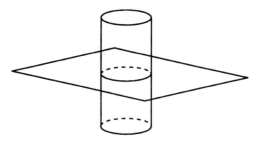

If a vertical plane were to intersect the cylinder, it would produce a different shape. The shapes formed when a plane cuts through a solid are called **cross sections** of the solid. You will intersect various solids with planes to determine the shapes that can be formed from different cross sections.

Investigating with Relational GeoSolids™

Predict the Results

Without looking at either the solids or drawings of them, predict the shape or shapes you will be able to form when intersecting a plane with each of the solids listed below. Write your predictions in the chart.

Predictions Chart: Shapes of Cross Sections

Relational GeoSolids Shape	Shape(s) of Cross Sections
Cube	
Rectangular Prism	
Triangular Prism	
Hexagonal Prism	
Cylinder	
Square Pyramid	
Triangular Pyramid	
Cone	
Sphere	

Procedure

1. Create a model for the first geometric solid listed in the Results Chart. First, grease the inside of the solid with nonstick cooking spray or vegetable oil. Then, straighten the outermost bend of a large paperclip. Bend the paper clip up 90° at the middle bend so that it can stand up on its own on the base created by the smaller, inside bend. Widen the angle of this small bend to create a wider *V*-shaped base.

Materials

For each pair of students:

▶ *1 Relational GeoSolids set*

▶ *A can of nonstick cooking spray or a small bottle of vegetable oil and a paper towel*

▶ *1 can of modeling clay*

▶ *3 1-ft. lengths of thread or dental floss*

▶ *A few large paper clips*

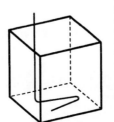

Investigating with Relational GeoSolids™

Remove the green base from the Relational GeoSolid. Put the *V*-shaped end of the paper clip in the solid and allow the other end to extend out of the top. Fill the solid with modeling clay. Then, carefully use the paper clip to pull the clay model out of the solid.

2. Use thread or dental floss to cut through the solid and divide it in two. Remember, the thread is simulating a plane, so be sure to cut through the solid in as straight a line as possible.

3. Look at the shape of the cross section. Draw or write the name of the shape in the Results Chart, next to the name of the geometric solid used. Your teacher might also ask you to record the orientation of the plane that produced each shape.

4. Put the clay solid back together as best as possible, then cut through it again at a different orientation. Record the shape formed by the intersection of the plane and the solid. Be specific in describing the shapes. For example, use the term *rhombus* instead of *parallelogram* if this term applies. Continue this process until you think you have found all the possible cross-sectional shapes for each solid.

5. Repeat steps 1 through 4 for each of the solids listed in the Results Chart.

Results Chart: Shapes of Cross Sections

Relational GeoSolids Shape	Shape(s) Formed
Large Cube	
Rectangular Prism	
Large Triangular Prism	
Hexagonal Prism	
Large Cylinder	
Square Pyramid	
Triangular Pyramid	
Cone	
Sphere	

Discussion Questions

1. Compare your predictions with your results.

    a. Do they match? If not, how are they different?

    b. Explain why your predictions differ from the results.

2. Look at the Results Chart above to answer the following questions.

    a. Which solids have a cross section in the shape of a circle?

    b. Which solids have a cross section in the shape of a rectangle?

    c. Which solids have a cross section in the shape of a triangle?

3. Look at your results for the prisms and the cylinder.

    a. What shape did you find in all of these solids?

    b. Why can this shape always be formed from a cross section of these solids?

    c. Would you expect the same results on an octagonal prism? Explain your answer.

    d. List all the shapes that could be formed by intersecting a plane with an octagonal prism.

4. Look at your results for the pyramids and the cone.

    a. What shape did you find on all of these solids?

    b. Why can this shape always be formed from a cross section of these solids?

    c. Would you expect the same results on a pentagonal pyramid? Explain your answer.

    d. List all the shapes that could be formed by intersecting a plane with a pentagonal pyramid.

Further Investigations

1. Make clay models or drawings of the various Relational GeoSolids and explore their possible lines of symmetry.

    a. Which geometric solid(s) has the greatest number of lines of symmetry? Explain why this is true.

    b. Which geometric solid(s) has the fewest number of lines of symmetry? Explain why this is true.

2. Biologists use the terms *radial symmetry* and *bilateral symmetry* to describe the body structure of organisms. Define each term and give examples of organisms with each type of symmetry.

3. Scientists often need to determine the cross-sectional area of a pipe or a blood vessel in order to determine the rate of flow of liquids traveling through them.

    a. Calculate the relevant cross-sectional areas of the small and large cylinders, as if they were pieces of pipes.

    b. If the velocity of the water were 6 inches per second, what volume of water would flow through each cross-section per second?

Investigating with Relational GeoSolids™

What Shapes Can You Make by Intersecting Planes with Solids?

Investigation 6

Objectives

- Determine the different shapes that are formed when different planes intersect various solids.

- Make generalizations about the types of shapes that can be formed from the intersections of a plane and a prism and a plane and a pyramid.

Getting Started
Ask students to define a *line*, a *plane*, and an *intersection*. Have students use pieces of paper to represent planes and their pencils to represent lines. Ask them to determine what is formed when a line intersects a plane. Demonstrate that a line or a point may be formed from the intersection of a line and a plane. Explain that students will investigate the different shapes formed when planes intersect various geometric solids.

Mathematical Review
Go over the review provided on the student pages. Be sure that students understand what a plane is, and explain to them how a taut string slicing through the clay represents a plane intersecting a solid.

Predict the Results
Remind students to make thoughtful predictions and not to change them as they work.

Procedure

1. Demonstrate how to use the vegetable oil or nonstick cooking spray to grease the mold. Then show them how to bend and position the large paper clip, which will be used to pull the clay out of the mold. Be sure to bend the paper clip so that it has a triangle at one end with a handle that extends straight up above the mold. Both the triangular base and the handle should set flush against the mold. Position the clip in the mold and pack the mold with clay. Then slowly pull the clay model out and carefully remove the paper clip. (For the pyramids, cone, and sphere the paper clip needs to be folded into a 2-dimensional V-shape with one side much longer than the other.)

2. Demonstrate how to use the thread or dental floss to simulate a plane cutting through a solid. Make sure students understand that the shape they are to describe is the flat surface formed along the cut.

3. The Results Chart shows the various shapes (including irregular shapes) students should get from cutting the molds of the different Relational GeoSolids. Students may or may not include points and lines as shapes that can be formed. Students may draw or write the names of the shapes, and you may want them to indicate the orientation of the plane that produced each shape.

4. Remind students to reconstruct the clay mold and to explore several ways the plane could intersect the solid.

5. Students will use the same clay to build and explore models of the other solids listed in the chart.

Results Chart: Shapes of Cross Sections

Relational GeoSolids Shape	Shape(s) Formed
Large cube	triangle*, square, rhombus, rectangle, pentagon, hexagon
Rectangular prism	triangle, square, parallelogram, rectangle, pentagon, hexagon
Large triangular prism	triangle, rectangle, trapezoid, pentagon
Hexagonal prism octagon	triangle, hexagon, rectangle, trapezoid, pentagon, heptagon,
Large cylinder	circle, ellipse, rectangle, parabola**
Square pyramid	triangle, square, trapezoid, kite-shaped quadrilateral, pentagon
Triangular pyramid	triangle, trapezoid, rectangle
Cone	triangle, circle, ellipse, parabola**

*Students may specify different types of triangles; you might even consider requiring them to do so.

**Note: Depending on the level and experience of the students, some shapes (*parabola* or *heptagon* for example) may be difficult for them to find. You may wish to assist them in discovering these particular shapes.

Investigation 6

What Shapes Can You Make by Intersecting Planes with Solids?

Discussion Questions

1a. Predictions and answers will vary. Students should, however, address whether their predictions match their results and how they are different.

1b. Answers will vary. For example, a student may say that the difference between her predictions and results was because she did not consider all of the different angles at which a plane may intersect a solid.

2a. The sphere, the cylinder, and the cone all have circular cross sections.

2b. All prisms (including the cube), the cylinder, and the square pyramid have rectangular cross sections.

2c. All pyramids and prisms and the cone have triangular cross sections.

3a. All prisms and the cylinder have rectangular cross sections.

3b. All of these solids have a pair of congruent bases and the sides are at right angles to the bases, so a rectangle is formed when a plane intersects the two bases.

3c. Yes. An octagonal prism has the same basic characteristics as other prisms, so a plane could cut through it to form a rectangle. (Students may explain their answers to 3b and 3c with a drawing.)

3d. A plane intersecting an octagonal prism could produce polygons with anywhere from 3 to 10 sides.

4a. All pyramids and the cone have triangular cross sections.

4b. All of these solids have a single vertex (an apex) at the top, and a base at the bottom, so a triangle is formed when a plane cuts through the top vertex (apex) and the base.

4c. Yes. A pentagonal pyramid has the same basic characteristics as other pyramids, so a plane could cut through it to form a triangle. (Students may explain their answers to 4b and 4c with a drawing.)

4d. A plane intersecting a pentagonal pyramid could produce the following shapes: triangles, trapezoids, pentagons, and hexagons.

Further Investigations

1a. The cone and the cylinders have the greatest number of lines of symmetry because they each have infinitely many diameters, so they have infinitely many lines of symmetry along each of their axes.

1b. The rectangular prism has the fewest number of lines of symmetry because it has the fewest number of congruent sides.

2. Radial symmetry—having multiple lines of symmetry along the same axis. A starfish has radial symmetry.

Bilateral symmetry—having or formed of just two symmetrical sides. A human has bilateral symmetry.

3a. Large cylinder—the interior diameter is about 2 inches, so the radius is about 1 inch. The cross-sectional area, therefore, is about $\pi(1 \text{ in.})^2 = 3.14 \text{ in.}^2$.

Small cylinder—the interior diameter is about 1 inch, so the radius is about 0.5 inch. The cross-sectional area, therefore, is about $\pi(0.5 \text{ in.})^2 = 0.785 \text{ in.}^2$.

3b. Large cylinder—the volume of water would be 3.14 in.^{2} × 6 in. = 18.84 in.^{3}.

Small cylinder—the volume of water would be 0.785 in.^{2} × 6 in. = 4.71 in.^{3}.

Investigation 7 : What Patterns Exist Among Vertices, Faces, and Edges?

Many patterns exist among the vertices, faces, and edges of solid figures. These relationships have been studied extensively by many brilliant minds, including René Descartes, Leonhard Euler, and William Rowan Hamilton. Some of the discoveries of these famous mathematicians concerning these patterns have proven useful in engineering and computer science, especially for determining the possible and most efficient paths for circuits.

Leonhard Euler
(1707–1783)

Euler did research on this very topic—finding relationships involving vertices, faces, and edges. Therefore, an important circuit pattern, the Euler Path, bears his name.

Topic of Investigation

Relationships among vertices, faces, and edges on solids

Questions to Investigate

▶ *How is the number of vertices related to the number of faces on a prism or a pyramid?*

▶ *How is the number of vertices related to the number of edges on a prism or a pyramid?*

Mathematical Review

A **prism** is a solid with two parallel bases.

Each **base** of a prism is a polygon. One base of each Relational GeoSolid prism is green.

The **lateral faces** of a prism are the flat, rectangular surfaces on the sides.

The term **faces** refers to the lateral faces and the bases of the prism.

The faces intersect to form segments called **edges**.

A **vertex** (plural, **vertices**) is a point on the solid where 3 edges intersect.

A **pyramid** is a solid with a single base.

Similar to a prism, the **base** of a pyramid is a polygon.

The **lateral faces** of a pyramid are its flat, triangular surfaces.

The term **faces** refers to the lateral faces and the base of a pyramid.

The **edges** of a pyramid are formed where the faces intersect.

A pyramid has **vertices** where the edges intersect.

A pyramid always has a single **vertex** opposite its base, which is called an **apex**.

In this investigation, you will be examining the number of vertices, faces, and edges on several prisms and pyramids. You will look for patterns and try to discover how the numbers of vertices, faces, and edges on a solid are related.

Predict the Results

Look at the list of geometric solids below. Without looking at either the actual solids or drawings of them, predict which shapes will fit the given criteria.

Cube   Rectangular Prism   Square Prism   Triangular Prism
Hexagonal Prism   Square Pyramid   Triangular Pyramid

Predictions Chart: Vertices, Faces, and Edges

Which Shape	Shape(s)
Has the largest number of faces?	
Has the least number of edges?	
Has the greatest ratio of vertices to faces?	
Has an equal number of vertices and faces?	
Has the least ratio of lateral faces to faces?	

Procedure

1. Examine each of the geometric solids listed in the Results Chart.

2. Count the number of vertices, lateral faces, total faces (lateral faces plus base or bases), and edges on each solid. Record your answers in the Results Chart.

Materials

For each pair of students:

▶ *1 Relational GeoSolids set*

Investigating with Relational GeoSolids™

Results Chart: Number of Vertices, Faces, and Edges in Each Geometric Solid

Relational GeoSolids Shape	Number of Vertices	Number of Lateral Faces	Total Number of Faces	Number of Edges
Cube				
Rectangular Prism				
Square Prism				
Triangular Prism				
Hexagonal Prism				
Square Pyramid				
Triangular Pyramid				

Investigating with Relational GeoSolids™

Discussion Questions

1. Compare your predictions with your results.

    a. Do they match? If not, how are they different?

    b. Explain why your predictions differ from the results.

2. Look at your results for the prisms.

    a. How is the number of lateral faces in each prism related to the number of vertices? Use examples to support your answer.

    b. How is the total number of faces in each prism related to the number of vertices? Use examples to support your answer.

    c. How is the number of edges in each prism related to the number of vertices? Use examples to support your answer.

    d. Use your results to determine the number of vertices, lateral faces, total number of faces, and edges in an octagonal prism.

3. Look at your results for the pyramids.

    a. How is the number of lateral faces in each pyramid related to the number of vertices? Use examples to support your answer.

    b. How is the total number of faces in each pyramid related to the number of vertices? Use examples to support your answer.

    c. How is the number of edges in each pyramid related to the number of vertices? Use examples to support your answer.

    d. Use your results to determine the number of vertices, lateral faces, total number of faces, and edges in a hexagonal pyramid.

Further Investigations

1. a. Do prisms always have an even number of vertices? Explain why they do or do not.

    b. Do pyramids always have an even number of vertices? Explain why they do or do not.

2. The number of edges on a prism is always a multiple of what number? Explain.

3. Based on the number of sides in a base, *b*, write rules or formulas for finding the number of vertices, faces, and edges for

    a. a prism

    b. a pyramid

4. Working in teams, research one of the three mathematicians mentioned in the introduction. Give a class presentation on his more important contributions to mathematics and science.

Objectives

- Discover the patterns among vertices, faces, and edges.

- Use mathematical language to explain these patterns.

- Use the patterns to determine the number of vertices, faces, and edges in unexplored solids.

Getting Started Ask students to define the terms *vertex*, *lateral face*, *base*, and *edge*. Also ask them the following questions: *How many bases does a prism have? How many bases does a pyramid have?*

Ensure that students understand that the lateral faces include only the side faces, whereas the total number of faces includes the lateral faces plus the base(s). Ensure that students realize that a pyramid has just one base, but a prism has two bases because both the top and the bottom of a prism are referred to as *bases*.

Mathematical Review As necessary, go over the review provided on the student pages. Be sure that students understand each of the terms.

Predict the Results Remind students to make thoughtful predictions and not to change them as they work.

Procedure

1. Tell students they can use either the large or small cube and either the large or small triangular pyramid for this activity.

2. Remind students to count the vertices, faces, and edges in a systematic way so that they do not lose track while they are counting. Also, remind them that both the top and bottom of a prism are bases and that the total number of faces equals the number of lateral faces plus the base(s).

Results Chart: Number of Vertices, Faces, and Edges in each Geometric Solid

Relational GeoSolids Shape	Number of Vertices	Number of Lateral Faces	Total Number of Faces	Number of Edges
Cube	8	4	6	12
Rectangular prism	8	4	6	12
Square prism	8	4	6	12
Triangular prism	6	3	5	9
Hexagonal prism	12	6	8	18
Square pyramid	5	4	5	8
Triangular pyramid	4	3	4	6

Discussion Questions

1a. Predictions and answers will vary. Students should, however, address whether their predictions match their results and how they are different.

1b. Answers will vary. For example, a student may indicate that she forgot to consider the lateral edges of the prisms in her predictions, so she predicted that the prisms would have fewer edges than they do.

2a. The number of lateral faces in a prism is half the number of vertices. For example, a rectangular prism has 8 vertices and 4 lateral faces, and a triangular prism has 6 vertices and 3 lateral faces.

2b. The total number of faces in a prism is half the number of vertices, plus 2. For example, a rectangular prism has 8 vertices and 6 total faces, and a triangular prism has 6 vertices and 5 total faces.

2c. The number of edges in a prism is half again the number of vertices. For example, a rectangular prism has 8 vertices and 12 edges, and a triangular prism has 6 vertices and 9 edges.

2d. An octagonal prism would have 16 vertices, 8 lateral faces, a total of 10 faces, and 24 edges.

3a. The number of lateral faces in a pyramid is 1 less than the number of vertices. For example, a square pyramid has 5 vertices and 4 lateral faces, and a triangular pyramid has 4 vertices and 3 lateral faces.

3b. The total number of faces in a pyramid is equal to the number of vertices. For example, a square pyramid has 5 vertices and a total of 5 faces, and a triangular pyramid has 4 vertices and a total of 4 faces.

3c. The number of edges in a pyramid is twice the number of vertices, minus 2 (or double 1 less than the number of vertices). For example, a square pyramid has 5 vertices and 8 edges $((2 \times 5) - 2)$, and a triangular pyramid has 4 vertices and 6 edges $((2 \times 4) - 2)$.

3d. A hexagonal pyramid would have 7 vertices, 6 lateral faces, a total of 7 faces, and 12 edges.

Further Investigations

1a. Yes, because their vertices are all located on their bases, and they have 2 bases. Any multiple of 2 is an even number.

1b. No, they can have either an even or odd number of vertices. A pyramid will have an even number of vertices only if its base has an odd number of sides.

2. On a prism, the number of edges is always a multiple of 3 because the number of edges equals 3 times the number of vertices on 1 base. (There are 2 congruent bases, each with the same number of vertices as edges, plus the edges connecting the 2 bases at the vertices.)

3a. prism:

number of vertices = $2b$

total number of faces = $b + 2$

number of edges = $3b$

3b. pyramid:

number of vertices = $b + 1$

total number of faces = $b + 1$

number of edges = $2b$

4. Student presentations will vary depending on the materials available to them and the additional instruction and guidance they receive from you regarding the requirements for their presentations.

Investigation 8: How Do You Find the Volumes of Prisms and Cylinders?

Volume has applications in many different fields, especially science, engineering, architecture, and construction. It is also useful in everyday life. For example, how many buckets of water are needed to fill an aquarium like that shown at the right? In this activity, you will determine the volumes of various prisms and cylinders, and explore the relationships among their formulas.

How many 1-gallon buckets are needed to fill a fish tank?

Topic of Investigation

Influences of dimensions of prisms and cylinders on volume

Questions to Investigate

▶ *How do you find the volume of prisms and cylinders?*

▶ *How do the dimensions of a solid affect its volume?*

▶ *How does the formula for the volume of a cylinder relate to the formula for the volume of a prism?*

Mathematical Review

Volume the capacity of a solid or the amount of space the solid occupies. In this investigation, you will find the volumes of different prisms and cylinders.

Prism a three-dimensional figure with two parallel, congruent polygons as bases and at least three rectangular faces.

Cylinder a three-dimensional figure similar to a prism, except its bases are congruent circles instead of polygons. Thus, a cylinder does not have lateral faces.

To determine the volumes of various prisms and cylinders, you will calculate the areas of the solids' bases. Some of the area formulas you may need are shown below.

Area of a circle = πr^2 ($\pi \cong 3.14$ and r = radius)

Area of a square = s^2 (s = length of a side)

Area of a rectangle = bh (b = length of the base and h = height)

Area of a triangle = $\frac{1}{2}bh$ (b = length of the base and h = height)

Investigating with Relational GeoSolids™

Predict the Results

Look at each of the solids listed in the table below. Without doing any calculations, predict how the volumes of these solids compare. Rank them according to volume, with 1 representing the greatest volume and 7 representing the least.

Predictions Chart: Volumes and Rankings

Relational GeoSolids Shape	Rankings by Volume (1 = greatest 7 = least)
Square Prism	
Rectangular Prism	
Small Triangular Prism	
Large Triangular Prism	
Small Cylinder	
Large Cylinder	
Large Cube	

Procedure

1. Using your ruler, measure the height of each geometric solid listed in the Results Chart to the nearest $\frac{1}{8}$ inch. Then determine the area of the base of the solid. Record your answers in the first and second columns.

2. Multiply the values in the first and second columns to determine the volume of each solid. Record your answers in the third column.

3. Rank the solids according to their volumes, with 1 representing the greatest volume and 7 representing the least. Record the rankings in the fourth column.

Materials

For each pair of students:

▶ *1 Relational GeoSolids set*

▶ *A customary or metric ruler*

▶ *A calculator*

Results Chart: Actual Volumes and Rankings

Relational GeoSolids Shape	Height (inches)	Area of Base (inches^2)	Volume (inches^3)	Rankings by Volume (1 = greatest 7 = least)
Square Prism				
Rectangular Prism				
Small Triangular Prism				
Large Triangular Prism				
Small Cylinder				
Large Cylinder				
Large Cube				

Discussion Questions

1. Compare your predictions with your results.

   a. Do they match? If not, how are they different?

   b. Explain why your predictions differ from the results.

   c. How did your estimates compare with your classmates' estimates?

2. Look at your Results Chart.

   a. In one sentence, summarize the measurements and the method you used to calculate the volumes of the solids.

   b. Why does this method for calculating volume work?

   c. Do you think you could find the volume of any prism or cylinder by using this method? Explain your thinking.

3. The formula for the volume of a cylinder is $V = \pi r^2 h$. How is this formula related to the method you used to determine the volumes of the cylinders and prisms?

Investigating with Relational GeoSolids™

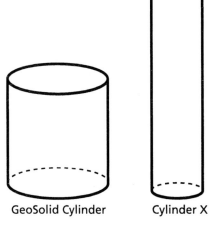

GeoSolid Cylinder   Cylinder X

4. Cylinder X is twice as tall as the large Relational GeoSolids cylinder, but its radius is only half as long.

   a. Which cylinder has the larger volume, Cylinder X or the large Relational GeoSolids cylinder? Explain.

   b. How tall would Cylinder X have to be in order to have the same volume as the large Relational GeoSolids cylinder? (Hint: Volume of Cylinder X = Volume of large cylinder. Solve for the height (*h*) of Cylinder X.) Explain.

   c. Which would have a greater effect on the volume of a cylinder—doubling its height or doubling the radius of its base? Explain.

Further Investigations

1. A rectangular box has three dimensions, length (*l*), width (*w*), and height (*h*).

   a. What would be the effect on the volume of the box if *l* was doubled, but the other dimensions remained the same?

   b. What would be the effect on the volume of the box if *l* and *w* were each doubled but *h* remained the same?

   c. What would be the effect on the volume of the box if *l*, *w*, and *h* were all doubled?

   d. What would be the effect on the volume of the box if *l*, *w*, and *h* were all tripled?

2. Determine the volume of the hexagonal prism using the same method you used for the other prisms. Explain all the steps you use to get your answer.

3. The science lab has a 36" wide × 18" deep × 20" high rectangular aquarium that needs to be filled. The students have a 12"-high cylindrical bucket with a 12"-diameter to fill the tank. If the aquarium contains 3" of gravel and the bucket is filled to a depth of 11", how many buckets of water will it take to fill the aquarium? Explain your strategy and show all necessary calculations.

How Do You Find the Volumes of Prisms and Cylinders? Investigation 8

Objectives

- Determine the volumes of various prisms and cylinders.

- Investigate how changing the dimensions of a prism or cylinder affects its volume.

Getting Started Ask students to define *volume;* make sure that they understand its concept. Ask students if they know how to figure out the volume of any solids. Students may know how to determine the volume of a rectangular prism by multiplying its three dimensions. Make sure students know what prisms and cylinders are. You may want to discuss the similarities and differences between various prisms and cylinders. To ascertain if students know what prisms and cylinders look like, consider having them point out examples of these solids in the classroom. In this activity, students will need to calculate the area of various plane figures, such as circles, squares, rectangles, and triangles. Ask students to try to recall how to calculate these areas, and spend some time reviewing the area formulas. This may lead to a discussion about the difference between area and volume. Make sure students understand the difference.

Mathematical Review As necessary, go over the review provided on the student pages, particularly the area formulas.

Predict the Results Remind students to make thoughtful predictions and not to change them as they do the work.

Procedure

1. Circulate among students to ensure that they are accurately measuring the dimensions of the solids to the nearest $\frac{1}{8}$". Make sure they calculate the area of each base, and do not just write down the dimensions.

2. Assure that students use the area of the base and the height of each solid to calculate its volume.

3. Check that students rank the solid with the greatest volume as 1 and the least volume as 7.

Results Chart: Actual Volumes and Rankings

Relational GeoSolids Shape	Height (inches)	Area of Base (inches²)	Volume (inches³)	Ranking by Volume (1 5 greatest 7 5 least)
Square prism	2.125	(1.125)(1.125) = 1.266	2.69	5
Rectangular prism	2.125	(2.125)(1.125) = 2.391	5.08	3
Small triangular prism	2.125	$\frac{1}{2}$(1.25)(1.125) = 0.703	1.49	7
Large triangular prism	2.125	$\frac{1}{2}$(2.25)(1.875) = 2.109	4.48	4
Small cylinder	2.125	(3.14)(0.5625)² = 0.994	2.11	6
Large cylinder	2.125	(3.14)(1.0625)² = 3.545	7.53	2
Large cube	2.125	(2.125)(2.125) = 4.516	9.60	1

Discussion Questions

1a. Predictions and answers will vary. Students should, however, address whether their predictions match their results and how they are different.

1b. Answers will vary. For example, students may say that they thought that the rectangular and large triangular prisms would have larger volumes than the large cylinder because they have corners.

1c. Answers will vary. For example, students should state whether their predictions were the same as or different from the other students.

2a. To determine the volume of each solid, you have to multiply the height of the solid by the area of one of its bases.

2b. Volume refers to how much space an object takes up. The area of the base represents how much space the base takes up, and the height represents how many times the base area is "piled up." When you multiply the area of the base by the height, you are figuring out how much space the bases that are "piled up" occupy.

2c. Yes. This method will work as long as you can determine the area of the base and the height of the prism or cylinder.

3. To determine the volume of a cylinder, you multiply the area of one base by the height. In a cylinder, the base is always a circle, which has an area of πr^2. So, the volume is πr^2 times height or $\pi r^2 h$.

4a. The large Relational GeoSolids cylinder has a larger volume. The volume of Cylinder X is $(3.14)(0.53125^2)(4.25) = 3.77$ inches^3, and the volume of the large cylinder is 7.53 inches^3.

4b. Cylinder X would have to be 4 times as tall as the large Relational GeoSolids cylinder, meaning it would be 8.5" tall. Then it would have the same volume as the large cylinder. The volume would be $(3.14)(0.53125^2)(8.5) = 7.53$ inches^3.

4c. Doubling the radius of the base would have a greater effect on volume because the radius is squared, whereas you multiply by the height just once. Doubling the radius of the base would increase the volume by a factor of 4.

Further Investigations

1a. If *l* were doubled, the volume of the rectangular box would be doubled.

1b. If *l* and *w* were each doubled, the volume of the rectangular box would be increased by a factor of 4.

1c. If *l*, *w*, and *h* were each doubled, the volume of the rectangular box would be increased by a factor of 8.

1d. If *l*, *w*, and *h* were each tripled, the volume of the rectangular box would be increased by a factor of 27.

2. First you have to measure the height of the prism, which is 2.125". Then you have to figure out the area of one base. The base is a hexagon that can be divided into 6 congruent triangles, each with a base of 1.00". The height of the hexagonal base is 1.875", so the height of each triangle would be 1.875" ÷ 2 = 0.9375". The area of each triangle, therefore, is $\frac{1}{2}(1.00")(0.9375") = 0.469$ inches^2.

Since there are 6 triangles in the hexagon, the area of the hexagonal base is (0.469 inches^2 × 6) or 2.81 inches^2. To find the volume of the prism, multiply the area of the base by the height, so the volume of the hexagonal prism is (2.81 inches^2)(2.125") = 5.97 inches^3 ≈ 6 inches^3.

3. To determine the volume of water needed in the aquarium, multiply the area of the base (36" × 18" = 648 inches^2) by the height of the water, less the gravel (20" − 3" = 17"), so the volume is 11,016 inches^3. To determine the volume of water in each bucket, multiply the area of the base (3.14 × (6")^2 = 113.04 inches^2) by the height of the water in the bucket (11"), so the volume is 1243.44 inches^3. To figure out how many buckets of water the students need, divide the volume of the aquarium by the volume of the bucket:

11,016 inches^3 ÷ 1243.44 inches^3 = 8.86

Thus, the students need 9 buckets of water.

Investigation 9: How Do the Volumes of Different Solids Relate?

Archimedes, the famous Greek mathematician and inventor, pondered such questions over 2,000 years ago. In his two-volume work, *On the Sphere and Cylinder*, he presented his discovery of the relationship between the volume of a sphere and the volume of a cylinder with the same diameter and height as the diameter of the sphere. Archimedes was so thrilled with his discovery of this relationship, he left instructions that his tomb should be marked with a sphere inscribed in a cylinder. In this activity, you will discover this relationship and many others among the volumes of different solids.

Topic of Investigation

Relationships among volumes of prisms, pyramids, cylinders, cones, and spheres

Questions to Investigate

▶ *What are the formulas for the volumes of prisms, pyramids, cylinders, cones, and spheres?*

▶ *How can you determine the volume of a prism, pyramid, cylinder, cone, or sphere without using a formula?*

▶ *How are the volumes of solids with bases that are the same shape and size related?*

▶ *Is the relationship between the volumes of the cone and the cylinder the same as the relationship between the volumes of the pyramid and the prism?*

Mathematical Review

Volume the capacity of a solid or the amount of space the solid occupies. In this investigation, you will determine how the volumes of prisms, cylinders, pyramids, cones, and spheres are related.

Pyramid a three-dimensional figure with a single base and at least three triangular faces. All of the lateral faces intersect at a vertex, known as an apex, opposite the base.

Cone a three-dimensional figure that is similar to a pyramid, except it has a circular base. Like a cylinder, a cone does not have any lateral faces.

Sphere a three-dimensional set of points that are the same distance from a center point.

Investigating with Relational GeoSolids™

Predict the Results

Without doing any calculations or experimentation, predict how the volumes for each of the following shapes are related to each other. Write a fraction in each blank predicting, for each pair, how much smaller the first solid is than the second solid.

Predictions Chart: Relationships among Volumes

Volume of the Rectangular Prism = _____ × Volume of the Large Cube

Volume of the Small Triangular Prism = _____ × Volume of the Hexagonal Prism

Volume of the Small Triangular Prism = _____ × Volume of the Large Triangular Prism

Volume of the Cone = _____ × Volume of the Large Cylinder

Volume of the Triangular Pyramid = _____ × Volume of the Large Triangular Prism

Volume of the Square Pyramid = _____ × Volume of the Large Cube

Volume of the Cone = _____ × Volume of the Hemisphere

Volume of the Sphere = _____ × Volume of the Large Cylinder

Procedure

1. Find the solids listed in the first row of the Results Chart. Fill the smaller of the two solids with water or rice.

2. Pour the water or rice from the smaller solid into the larger solid. Repeat until the larger solid is filled. The volume of the smaller solid is what fraction of the volume of the larger solid? Write that fraction in the appropriate blank in the Results Chart.

3. Repeat steps 1 and 2 to compare the volumes of each pair of solids listed in the Results Chart.

Materials

For each pair of students:

▶ *1 Relational GeoSolids set*

▶ *Water or rice*

▶ *A customary or metric ruler*

Results Chart: Relationships Among Volumes

Volume of the Rectangular Prism = _____ × Volume of the Large Cube

Volume of the Small Triangular Prism = _____ × Volume of the Hexagonal Prism

Volume of the Small Triangular Prism = _____ × Volume of the Large Triangular Prism

Volume of the Cone = _____ × Volume of the Large Cylinder

Volume of the Triangular Pyramid = _____ × Volume of the Large Triangular Prism

Volume of the Square Pyramid = _____ × Volume of the Large Cube

Volume of the Cone = _____ × Volume of the Hemisphere

Volume of the Sphere = _____ × Volume of the Large Cylinder

Discussion Questions

1. Compare your predictions with your results.

   a. Do they match? If not, how are they different?

   b. Explain why your predictions differ from the results.

   c. How did you make your predictions? Explain your thinking.

2. Look at your Results Chart.

   a. If the formula for the volume of a cylinder is $V = \pi r^2 h$, what is the formula for the volume of a cone with the same radius and height? Explain your thinking.

   b. If the formula for the volume of a sphere is $V = \frac{4}{3} r^3$, what is the formula for the volume of a hemisphere with the same radius? Explain your thinking.

3. a. How are the volumes of a prism and a pyramid that have the same height and congruent bases related?

   b. Do you think the relationship between the volumes of a cylinder and a cone with the same radius and height would be the same as the relationship above? Explain your reasoning.

4. Look at the relationship between the volumes of the small and large triangular prisms and the relationship between the volume of the small triangular prism and the hexagonal prism.

   a. Why did you get these results?

   b. Use these results to predict the relationship between the volume of the small cube and the large cube.

Further Investigations

1. Which two solids have the same volume? Use the formulas for the volumes of these solids to explain why they have the same volume.

2. Theater A sells popcorn in prism-shaped boxes at $2.50 a box. Theater B sells popcorn in pyramid-shaped boxes for $1.00 a box. The bases and heights of both popcorn boxes are the same.

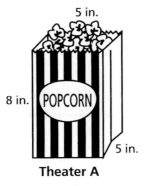

Theater A

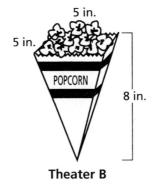

Theater B

   a. Which theater offers the better deal on popcorn? Explain your thinking.

   b. Keeping the shapes of the boxes the same, design a new but different popcorn box for one of the theaters, so that the boxes at both theaters will hold the same amount of popcorn.

3. A single scoop of frozen yogurt has a diameter of 3 inches.

   a. If a waffle cone has a 3-inch diameter and a 6-inch height, will a single scoop of frozen yogurt that is melting in the sun overflow the cone? Explain why or why not.

   b. If a waffle cone has a 4-inch diameter and a 6-inch height, would a double scoop of frozen yogurt that is melting in the sun overflow the cone? Explain why or why not.

How Do the Volumes of Different Solids Relate? Investigation 9

Objectives

- Determine the relationships between the volumes of prisms, pyramids, cylinders, cones, and spheres

- Use the relationships among the volumes of some solids to predict the relationships among the volumes of other solids

Getting Started
Ask students to define *volume*, making sure they understand the concept of volume. Discuss with students the different ways to determine volume, i.e., using formulas, using water displacement, and measuring the amount a solid holds. Explain that students will be filling solids with water or rice in this activity. To discover

the relationships among the volumes of these solids, they will compare the amounts that different solids hold. Ask students if they know the relationships among the volumes of any of the solids. For example, they may know that the volume of the hemisphere is half the volume of the sphere. Tell students that they will discover many other relationships that are not as obvious as that one.

Mathematical Review
As necessary, go over the review provided on the student pages. Make sure students can identify the solids by name.

Predict the Results
Remind students to make thoughtful predictions and not to change them as they work.

Procedure

1. Circulate among students to ensure that they are being careful not to spill as they pour the water or rice from one solid to another. Explain that spillage will affect the outcome.

2. Encourage students to estimate the fraction of the larger solid that is filled with the contents of the smaller solid as accurately as possible. When students make their estimates, they may want to use rulers to determine the appropriate fractions. For example, since the large triangular

prism is about 2 inches tall and the small triangular prism will fill the large one to about $\frac{1}{2}$ inch, the fraction that is filled is $\frac{1}{4}$. You may also want students to make a sketch to show the fraction of each solid that is filled. Time permitting, students could also determine the actual volume of each solid by measuring its capacity with water and a graduated cylinder. They could then check their estimates against their actual measurements.

Results Chart: Relationships Among Volumes

Volume of the Rectangular Prism = $\frac{1}{2}$ × Volume of the Large Cube	
Volume of the Small Triangular Prism = $\frac{1}{6}$ × Volume of the Hexagonal Prism	
Volume of the Small Triangular Prism = $\frac{1}{4}$ × Volume of the Large Triangular Prism	
Volume of the Cone = $\frac{1}{3}$ × Volume of the Large Cylinder	
Volume of the Triangular Pyramid = $\frac{1}{3}$ × Volume of the Large triangular Prism	
Volume of the Square Pyramid = $\frac{1}{3}$ × Volume of the Large Cube	
Volume of the Cone = 1 × Volume of the Hemisphere	
Volume of the sphere = $\frac{2}{3}$ × Volume of the Large Cylinder	

Discussion Questions

1a. Predictions and answers will vary. Students should, however, address whether their predictions match their results and how they are different.

1b. Answers will vary. For example, students may not have realized that the volume of the cone is $\frac{1}{3}$ the volume of the cylinder, or that the volume of the square pyramid is $\frac{1}{3}$ the volume of the large cube. They may not have predicted that the hemisphere and the cone have the same volume.

1c. Answers will vary. For example, students may explain that they tried to estimate how many of the smaller solid in each pair would fit inside the larger solid.

2a. The formula for the volume of a cone should be $V = (\frac{1}{3})\pi r^2 h$ because the volume of the cone is $\frac{1}{3}$ the volume of the cylinder.

2b. The formula for the volume of a hemisphere should be $V = (\frac{2}{3})\pi r^3$ because the volume of the hemisphere is $\frac{1}{2}$ the volume of the sphere.

3a. The volume of the pyramid is $\frac{1}{3}$ the volume of the prism.

3b. Student answers will vary; however, students may intuitively hypothesize that the volume of the cone is $\frac{1}{3}$ the volume of the cylinder. Students may think that the relationship is the same because just like a prism and a pyramid, the base of a cone with the same base radius and height as a cylinder is congruent to the two bases of the cylinder. Also, both the prism and the cylinder have two bases, but the pyramid and the cone have only one base and a single vertex, or apex.

4a. The volume of the small triangular prism is $\frac{1}{4}$ the volume of the large triangular prism because 4 of the small triangular prisms could be put together to form the large triangular prism, as shown. The volume of the small triangular prism is $\frac{1}{6}$ the volume of the hexagonal prism because 6 of the small triangular prisms could be put together to form the hexagonal prism, as shown here.

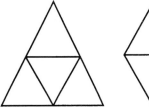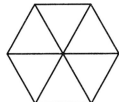

4b. The volume of the small cube should be $\frac{1}{8}$ the volume of the large cube because 8 small cubes could be put together to form the large cube.

Further Investigations

1. The hemisphere and the cone have the same volume. The formula for the volume of a hemisphere is $V = (\frac{2}{3})\pi r^3$ and the formula for the volume of a cone is $V = (\frac{1}{3})\pi r^2 h$. Since the height of the cone is two times the radius of both solids, you can think of the h in the cone formula as $2r$. Then, the volume of the cone is $(\frac{1}{3})\pi r^2(2r) = (\frac{2}{3})\pi r^3$, which is the same as the volume of the hemisphere.

2a. Theater A offers the better deal because the prism-shaped box has 3 times as much popcorn in it. You can buy 3 pyramid-shaped boxes from Theater B to get the same amount of popcorn as you get in the prism-shaped box, but you will pay $3.00 instead of $2.50.

2b. Student answers will vary. For example, one dimension of the pyramid-shaped box could be three times the corresponding dimension in the prism-shaped box. The pyramid-shaped box could have a base that is 5 inches by 5 inches with a height of 27 inches. Thus, both boxes have a volume of 225 inches^3.

3a. No, the yogurt will just fill the cone because the volume of the yogurt ($V = (\frac{4}{3})\pi(1.5 \text{ inches})^3 = 14.14 \text{ inches}^3$) is the same as the volume of the cone ($V = (\frac{1}{3})\pi(1.5 \text{ inches})^2(6 \text{ inches}) = 14.14 \text{ inches}^3$).

3b. Yes, the yogurt would overflow. The volume of the yogurt is twice as large as before (28.27 inches^3), but the volume of the cone is not ($V = (\frac{1}{3})\pi(2 \text{ inches})^2(6 \text{ inches}) = 25.13 \text{ inches}^3$).

Investigation 10: How Do Metric and Customary Units Relate?

Officially, the metric system was first adopted in France in 1799, although European scientists had been discussing the development of a new, more rational, uniform system of measurement for more than a century before that.

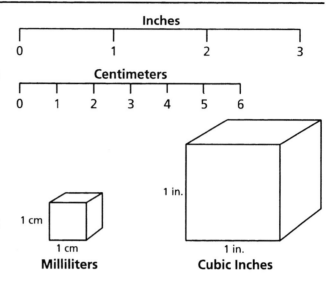

Milliliters

Cubic Inches

The metric system has become the primary system of measurement throughout the world. The United States was a signatory to the Metric Convention of 1875. In 1971, an investigative report presented to Congress recommended that we should convert to the metric system by the early 1980s. To date, however, in the United States, the metric system is firmly established only in specific professional fields: the automotive industry, science, medicine, electronics, photography, and optometry. Regardless of its limited use in the United States, in order to effectively communicate and trade with other nations, we must be able to understand and use the metric system.

Topic of Investigation

Relationships between metric and customary units

Questions to Investigate

▶ *How are metric and customary units related?*

▶ *How do you convert linear measurements to cubic measurements?*

▶ *How do cubic measurements relate to liquid measurements of volume?*

Mathematical Review

The basic unit of measurement for length in the metric system is the **meter** (m); the basic unit of measurement for liquid volume is the **liter** (L). The prefix **centi-** means $\frac{1}{100}$ and the prefix **milli-** means $\frac{1}{1000}$. Thus, a **centimeter** equals $\frac{1}{100}$ of a meter and a **millimeter** equals $\frac{1}{1000}$ of a meter. Volume is measured in cubic units, unless the volume is expressed in units of liquid volume, such as in **milliliters** (mL) and **liters** (L). In this activity, you will determine volumes in both metric and customary units. Thus, you will need to use the following equivalents in this activity:

$$1 \text{ cm} = \tfrac{1}{100}\text{m}, \ 1 \text{ mm} = \tfrac{1}{10}\text{cm}, \ 1 \text{ in.} = 2.54 \text{ cm},$$
$$1 \text{ cm}^3 = 1 \text{ mL, and } 1{,}000 \text{ mL} = 1 \text{ L}$$

When converting areas or volumes to different units of measurement, remember that the **values** of the equivalent measurements must be squared and cubed in addition to the units. For example, an area of 1 in.^{2} is equivalent to 6.45 cm^2, not 2.54 cm^2, as explained below.

$$1 \text{ in.} = 2.54 \text{ cm, so } (1 \text{ in.})^2 = (2.54 \text{ cm})^2$$

because both sides of the equation must be squared. Thus,

$$1 \text{ in.}^2 = (2.54 \text{ cm})(2.54 \text{ cm}) = 6.45 \text{ cm}^2.$$

Similarly, the volume 1 in.^{3} is equivalent to 16.39 cm^3.

Investigating with Relational GeoSolids™

Predict the Results

Consider the geometric solids listed below. Without measuring the solids or looking at the cubic centimeter (cm³) blocks, predict how many whole cubic centimeter blocks will fit in each solid. Also, predict how many milliliters (mL) of water each solid can hold. Write your predictions below.

Predictions Chart: How Many Cubic Centimeter Blocks and Milliliters Can Each Hold?

Relational GeoSolids Shape	Number of Whole Cubic Centimeter Blocks	Number of Milliliters of Water
Large Cube		
Rectangular Prism		
Square Prism		
Small Cube		

Procedure

1. Measure the dimensions of each solid listed in the Results Chart on the next page to the nearest $\frac{1}{8}$ inch. Change mixed numbers to decimals and record your results in row 1.

2. Calculate the volume ($l \times w \times h$) of each solid in cubic inches. Record your results in row 2.

3. Convert each volume from cubic inches to cubic centimeters. Record your results in row 3.

4. Measure the dimensions of each solid listed in the Results Chart to the nearest $\frac{1}{2}$ centimeter. Record your results in row 4.

5. Calculate the volume of each solid in cubic centimeters. Record your results in row 5.

6. Place cubic centimeter blocks in rows inside of each Relational GeoSolid to determine how many blocks will fit in the solid. If another block almost fits in a row, you may squish the blocks together very slightly, but do not greatly deform them. Record your results in row 6.

7. Fill the large cube with water. Pour the water from the cube into the graduated cylinder to determine the volume of the cube in milliliters. Record your results in row 7. Repeat for the other three solids.

Materials

For each pair of students:

▶ *1 Relational GeoSolids set*

▶ *A metric ruler and a customary ruler*

▶ *A set of foam or ManipuLite® cubic centimeter blocks*

▶ *1 graduated cylinder (marked in 2 mL increments)*

▶ *Water*

▶ *A funnel (optional) and a cafeteria tray (optional)*

Results Chart: Volumes of Solids in Cubic Inches, Cubic Centimeters, and Milliliters

Relational GeoSolids Shape	Large Cube	Rectangular Prism	Square Prism	Small Cube
Dimensions (inches)				
Calculated Volume (inches^3)				
Volume Converted from inches^3 to cm^3				
Dimensions (cm)				
Calculated Volume (cm^3)				
Number of Whole cm^3 Blocks				
Volume (mL)				

Discussion Questions

1. Compare your predictions with your results.

    a. Do your predictions match your results? If not, how are they different?

    b. Explain why your predictions differ from your results.

2. Look at your Results Chart.

    a. Compare your results for the volumes of each solid obtained by converting inches^3 to cm^3, by calculating cm^3 from cm measurements, and by determining the number of mL of water each solid holds. Are they approximately the same? Why or why not?

    b. Compare your results for the volumes obtained by filling the solids with whole cubic centimeter blocks and by filling them with water. Are they approximately the same? Why or why not?

3. A shipping box has a volume (capacity) of 2700 inches^3. What other information would you need to determine the number of 3" × 3" × 3" boxes that would fit in the shipping box? Explain.

Investigating with Relational GeoSolids™

4. Consider the advantages and disadvantages of the different methods for determining volume. Which method would you recommend using to accurately determine the volume (capacity) of a cylinder? Explain.

5. The ratio of the volume of the square pyramid to the volume of the large cube is 1:3. Use this ratio and your results for the large cube to determine the volume of the square pyramid in cm^3. Explain. Show your work.

6. What is the approximate volume (capacity) of a 6" x 6" x 6" cube in milliliters? (Assume that the material used to make up the surface of the cube is very thin.) Show your work.

Further Investigations

When the Metric System was established at the end of the 18th century, the following units were defined:

1. One gram was made equal to the mass of 1 cm^3 of water (at the temperature of its maximum density of 4°C (39.2°F). About how many grams of water would a 2" x 3" x 4" rectangular prism hold? (Assume that the material used to make up the surface of the cube is very thin.) Explain your thinking.

2. A liter was defined as the volume of a 10 cm × 10 cm × 10 cm cube. Use the equivalents in the Mathematical Review to prove that a cube with these dimensions contains 1 liter.

3. A platinum cylinder, known as the Kilogram of the Archives, was the standard for 1,000 grams. Platinum has a density of 21.45 g/cm^3 (at 20°C, which is approximately room temperature).

   a. What would be the radius of the cylinder if its height were 5 cm?

   b. What would be the height of the cylinder if its radius were 5 cm?

Objectives

- Investigate the relationship among metric and customary units.
- Investigate the relationship among different units of volume.
- Convert linear measurements to cubic measurements.

Getting Started
Ask students which item in each of the following pairs of units is larger:

1 centimeter or 1 inch? [1 inch]

1 meter or 1 yard? [1 meter]

1 gram or 1 ounce? [1 ounce]

1 kilogram or 1 pound? [1 kilogram]

1 liter or 1 quart? [1 liter, by a slight amount]

1 milliliter or 1 cubic inch? [1 inch^3]

1 milliliter or 1 cubic centimeter? [equal]

Explain to students that they will explore how some of the metric and customary units relate, how metric units relate to each other, how to convert units of volume, and different methods for measuring volume.

Mathematical Review
Go over the review provided on the student pages. Be sure that students understand each of the terms, how to use equivalents to convert units, and how to find the volume of a rectangular prism.

Predict the Results
Remind students to make thoughtful predictions and not to change them as they work.

Procedure

1. Circulate among students to ensure that they understand the task and that they measure the solids to the nearest $\frac{1}{8}$ inch. If necessary, provide a review of how to change mixed numbers to decimals.

2. Encourage students to double-check their calculations because they will use the results in the next step.

3. Remind students that they cannot simply multiply the volume in cubic inches by 2.54. Rather, they must multiply the volumes by the cube of 2.54 because they are converting volumes.

4. Remind students to measure the dimensions to the nearest $\frac{1}{2}$ cm.

5. Students will likely find it easier to calculate the volumes if they use decimals instead of fractions in the dimensions.

6. When filling the solids with cubic centimeter blocks, students are permitted to squish the blocks very slightly if another block almost fits in a row, but they should not greatly deform the blocks. The only solid for which they may squeeze the blocks in, therefore, is the large cube.

7. Ensure that students pour all the water from each solid into the graduated cylinder and that they correctly read the measurements on the graduated cylinder.

Results Chart: Volumes of Solids in Cubic Inches, Cubic Centimeters, and Milliliters

Relational GeoSolids Shape	Large Cube	Rectangular Prism	Square Prism	Small Cube
Dimensions (inches)	$2\frac{1}{8} \times 2\frac{1}{8} \times 2\frac{1}{8}$	$2\frac{1}{8} \times 2\frac{1}{8} \times 1\frac{1}{8}$	$2\frac{1}{8} \times 1\frac{1}{8} \times 1\frac{1}{8}$	$1\frac{1}{8} \times 1\frac{1}{8} \times 1\frac{1}{8}$
Calculated Volume (inches^3)	9.6	5.1	2.7	1.4
Volume Converted from in.^{3} to cm^3	157.3	83.3	44.1	23.3
Dimensions (cm)	$5.5 \times 5.5 \times 5.5$	$5.5 \times 5.5 \times 3$	$5.5 \times 3 \times 3$	$3 \times 3 \times 3$
Calculated Volume (cm^3)	166.4	90.75	49.5	27
Number of Whole cm^3 Blocks	125	50	20	8
Volume (mL)	123	61	30	16

Discussion Questions

1a. Predictions and answers will vary. Students should, however, address whether their predictions match their results, and how they are different.

1b. Answers will vary. For example, a student may indicate that her predictions differ from her results because she didn't consider the problem of fitting the whole cm^3 blocks into the solids with dimensions of 2.5 cm.

2a. Answers will vary depending upon students' measurements. Although students might say that some of the measurements are not similar, their answers should be somewhat like the following:

"Yes, they are basically similar, except for very minor differences among the volumes determined for the small cube, and somewhat larger differences between the volumes determined for the large cube. These differences are due to rounding to the nearest $\frac{1}{8}$ inch and to the nearest $\frac{1}{2}$ cm, as well as measuring inside versus outside volumes."

2b. Answers will vary, but they should be similar to the following:

"Only the volumes for the large cube are similar, because the other solids have one or more dimensions of 2.5 cm, and whole cm^3 blocks cannot be used to completely fill the other solids."

3. The needed information is the dimensions of the box, especially whether the dimensions are all multiples of 3.

4. Answers will vary. Students should choose, however, either accurately measuring the dimensions of the cylinder and calculating the volume, or filling the cylinder with water to determine its capacity in mL. The disadvantage of measuring the dimensions of the solid is that the capacity will likely be overestimated, unless the thickness of the plastic is taken into account. The disadvantage of the water method is that it is difficult to get rid of all the air bubbles, so the capacity is more likely to be underestimated. Using blocks would not work, because a cylinder is round, not square.

5. Answers may vary slightly based on students' results and the measurement they choose to use for the volume. If they use 125 cm^3 as the volume of the large cube, however, the volume of the square pyramid is about 42 cm^3 ($\frac{125 \text{ cm}^3}{3} = 41.7 \text{ cm}^3$).

6. The volume of a 6-inch cube is about 3,540 mL, because (6 inches)^3(2.54 cm/inch)^3 = 216(16.38) cm$^3 \approx$ 3,540 cm^3.

Further Investigations

1. A 2"× 3"× 4" rectangular prism would hold about 393.1 grams of water, because 2"(3")(4")(2.54 cm/inch)^3 = 393.1 cm^3, and the density of water is 1 g/cm^3.

2. A 10 cm × 10 cm × 10 cm cube has a volume of 1,000 cm^3. Since 1 cm^3 equals 1 mL, the cube has a volume of 1,000 mL, which equals 1 liter (L).

3a. The radius of the cylinder would be about 1.72 cm, because
πr^2(5 cm)(21.45 g/cm^3) = 1,000 g
(336.9 g/cm^2)r^2 = 1,000 g
r^2 = 2.97 cm^2
r = 1.72 cm

3b. The height of the cylinder would be about 0.59 cm, because
πh(5 cm)^2(21.45 g/cm^3) = 1,000 g
(1,684.7 g/cm)h = 1,000 g
h = 0.59 cm

Investigation 11: How Can an Object Have Two Different Volumes?

A hollow solid, such as a Relational GeoSolids shape, has two volumes—an inside one and an outside one. To find the inside volume of a solid, you will determine the amount of water the solid can hold. To measure the outside volume of a solid, you will use a technique called *water displacement,* much like Archimedes, the famous Greek mathematician, used to help him determine the amount of gold and silver in King Hieron's crown. The famous story of Archimedes leaping excitedly from his bath, running naked through the town, shouting "Eureka!" ("I have found it.") when he figured out how to solve the problem, is probably apocryphal. In any case, water displacement is a very useful method for finding the volumes of other irregularly shaped objects, such as rocks.

Eureka!

Topic
of Investigation

Variation between the inside volume and the outside volume of solids

Questions
to Investigate

▶ *Why is there a difference between the inside volume and the outside volume of a solid?*

▶ *What does the difference between the inside volume and the outside volume of a solid represent?*

▶ *Which solids have the greatest/least difference between their inside and outside volumes?*

▶ *How do the size and shape of a solid affect the difference between its inside and outside volumes?*

Mathematical Review

Volume How much a solid can hold, or how much space it takes up. The amount a solid can hold, its *capacity,* may be referred to as its **inside volume**. You will determine the inside volume of a solid by measuring how much liquid it takes to fill the solid.

How much space the solid takes up may be referred to as its **outside volume**. You will determine the outside volume of each solid using water displacement by measuring how much the level of water in a beaker changes when a solid is immersed in it.

You will determine the difference between the inside and outside volumes for each solid and then calculate the percentage of volume lost due to the thickness of the plastic. To determine the percentage of volume lost, you will divide each difference by the outside volume of that solid and multiply by 100.

Investigating with Relational GeoSolids™

Predict the Results

Examine each of the geometric solids listed below. Rank them according to the percentage of volume you think will be lost due to the thickness of the plastic, with 1 representing the greatest loss and 10 representing the least.

Predictions Chart: Volume Lost Due to Thickness of Plastic

Relational GeoSolids Shape	Rankings by Percentage of Volume Lost (1 = greatest 10 = least)
Large Cube	
Small Cube	
Rectangular Prism	
Square Prism	
Small Triangular Prism	
Small Cylinder	
Square Pyramid	
Triangular Pyramid	
Cone	
Sphere	

Procedure

1. Remove the stopper from the green base of the first solid listed in the Results Chart. Fill the solid with water and replace the stopper. Make sure that the water will not leak out.

Hint
▶ Ensure that there are no large air bubbles inside the solid. Thoroughly dry the outside of the solid.

Materials

For each pair of students:
▶ *1 Relational GeoSolids set*
▶ *One 1 L beaker marked in 10 mL increments*
▶ *One 100 mL graduated cylinder marked in 2 mL increments*
▶ *Water*
▶ *A customary ruler*
▶ *A calculator (optional)*
▶ *A funnel (optional) and a cafeteria tray (optional)*

2. Pour 400 mL of water into the beaker. Immerse the solid in the beaker of water and let it sink to the bottom. Then, measure the level of water in the beaker to the nearest 5 mL. Subtract 400 mL from this final measurement to determine the outside volume of the solid. Record your results in the first column of the Results Chart.

3. To measure the inside volume of the same solid, remove the solid from the beaker of water. Carefully remove the green stopper from the base of the solid and pour the water into the graduated cylinder. Measure the amount of water to the nearest 1 mL. Record your results in the second column of the Results Chart.

4. Repeat steps 1 through 3 for each solid in the Results Chart. Make sure you always start with 400 mL of water in the beaker.

5. Subtract the inside volume from the outside volume of each solid. Record your results in the third column of the Results Chart.

6. Determine the percentage of volume lost due to plastic for each solid. Divide each difference by the outside volume for that solid and multiply by 100. Record your results in the fourth column of the Results Chart.

7. Rank the solids according to the percentage of volume lost due to the plastic, with 1 representing the greatest percentage of loss and 10 representing the least percentage of loss. Record your results in the last column of the Results Chart.

Results Chart: Measuring Two Different Volumes

Relational GeoSolids Shape	Outside Volume (in mL)	Inside Volume (in mL)	Difference (in mL)	Percentage of Volume Lost	Rankings by Percentage Loss (1 = greatest 10 = least)
Large Cube					
Small Cube					
Rectangular Prism					
Square Prism					
Small Triangular Prism					
Small Cylinder					
Square Pyramid					
Triangular Pyramid					
Cone					
Sphere					

Discussion Questions

1. Compare your predictions with your results.

    a. Do they match? If not, how are they different?

    b. Explain why your predictions differ from your results.

2. Look at your Results Chart.

    a. Which solid has the greatest difference between its inside volume and its outside volume?

    b. Which solid has the greatest percentage of volume lost?

    c. Are your answers to part a and part b the same or different? Explain.

3. Use your ruler to measure the dimensions of the small cube and large cube. Measure each dimension to the nearest $\frac{1}{8}$ inch.

    a. Calculate the volumes of the small and large cubes in cubic inches by multiplying the length × the width × the height.

    b. Convert these volume measurements from cubic inches to milliliters by multiplying each result by 16.

    c. Compare these volume measurements to the volumes of the small cube and the large cube you measured using water. Are they more similar to the inside or the outside volume measurements? Explain.

4. Provide an example of a real life situation where it is important to be able to distinguish between inside and outside volume. Explain.

Further Investigations

1. Choose a number of irregularly shaped objects, such as rocks, and measure the outside volume.

    a. Look at the objects and predict their outside volumes by comparing them to the Relational GeoSolids. Your predictions should be in milliliters.

    b. Estimate the volume of each object, using a ruler and the formulas for the solids to which your objects are most similar. Estimate the volumes in cubic inches.

    c. Use water displacement to measure the outside volumes of your objects.

    d. How close were your estimates to the actual volumes?

2. The sphere and the rectangular prism have similar outside volumes, but the percentage of volume lost is different for the two solids.

    a. What factors affect the percentage of volume lost?

    b. Explain why the percentages are different for these two solids.

Investigating with Relational GeoSolids™

Objectives

• Measure the inside and outside volumes of various geometric solids.

• Examine how the difference between the inside volume and the outside volume of a solid relates to the solid's size and shape.

Getting Started Ask students to first define volume, then to explain how an object could have more than one volume. You may want to demonstrate and/or have students explore volume by filling objects with water, rice, sand, salt, etc. Students can compare the volumes of solids by measuring how much of the substance each one holds. Ensure students know how to read the measurements. Also, point out that they will be reading between the markings on the beaker and graduated cylinder in order to get accurate measurements. They will be measuring to the nearest 5 milliliters in the beaker and to the nearest milliliter in the graduated cylinder.

Note: This activity may take longer than one class period. If time constraints exist, we suggest allowing students to divide the work between two groups (5 solids each) and share the results with one another.

Mathematical Review As necessary, go over the review provided on the student pages. Be sure that students understand the difference between inside and outside volume.

Predict the Results Remind students to make thoughtful predictions and to not change them as they work.

Procedure

1. Demonstrate how to measure the inside volume and the outside volume of one of the Relational GeoSolids™. You may want to use one of the solids that will not be used in this investigation, e.g., the large cylinder. Explain the importance of filling each solid completely with water, eliminating air bubbles as much as possible to avoid inaccurate measurements for inside volume. Remind students to be careful not to spill any water when pouring the water from each solid into the graduated cylinder. To avoid inaccurate outside volume measurements, remind students to verify that the beaker has 400 mL of water and to dry the outside of each solid before immersing it in the water. They may need to replace water in the beaker before measuring each solid.

2. Make sure students are correctly determining the difference in volume for each solid.

3. Be sure that students understand how to determine the percentage of volume lost for each solid. Students may divide the difference by the inside volume instead of the outside volume.

Results Chart: Measuring Two Different Volumes

Relational GeoSolids™ Shape	Outside Volume (in mL)	Inside Volume (in mL)	Difference	Percentage of Volume Lost	Ranking by Percentage Lost (1 5 greatest 10 5 least)
Large Cube	155 mL	124 mL	31 mL	20%	9
Small Cube	25 mL	14 mL	11 mL	44%	2
Rectangular Prism	80 mL	62 mL	18 mL	22.5%	8
Square Prism	45 mL	30 mL	15 mL	33.3%	4
Small Triangular Prism	25 mL	13 mL	12 mL	48%	1
Small Cylinder	35 mL	24 mL	11 mL	31.4%	7
Square Pyramid	65 mL	44 mL	21 mL	32.3%	5
Triangular Pyramid	30 mL	19 mL	11 mL	36.7%	3
Cone	50 mL	34 mL	16 mL	32%	6
Sphere	80 mL	66 mL	14 mL	17.5%	10

Discussion Questions

1a. Predictions and answers will vary. Students should, however, address whether their predictions match their results and how they are different.

1b. Answers will vary. For example, students may say that they thought the larger solids would lose a larger percentage of volume and the smaller solids would lose a smaller percentage of volume.

2a. The large cube has the largest difference between its inside and outside volumes.

2b. The small triangular prism has the greatest percentage of volume lost due to the plastic.

2c. The answers are different. Even though the large cube has the largest difference in volume, it doesn't have the largest percentage loss. Overall, the small triangular prism lost less volume than the cube, but the percentage of its total volume lost is larger because it has less volume than the cube. (It has lost a relatively larger amount of water.)

3a. The volume of the large cube is 9.60 inches^3 $[(2.125)^3]$ and the volume of the small cube is 1.42 inches^3 $[(1.125)^3]$.

3b. The volume of the large cube is 153.53 mL and the volume of the small cube is 22.78 mL.

3c. The measurements are more similar to the outside volume measurements. When we measure dimensions with a ruler, we measure from outside edge to outside edge and do not account for the thickness of the plastic.

4. Answers will vary. Sample response:

"If you were packing a box with food and wanted to know how much room you had inside the box, you would need to distinguish between its inside and outside volumes. If you measured the box's outside dimensions and multiplied to determine the volume, your calculation would not be accurate. The thickness of the cardboard would take away some of the packing room inside the box. If you wanted to know how much space the box would take up after it is packed, however, you would need to know its outside volume."

Further Investigations

1a. Student answers will vary, depending upon the object(s) they choose to measure. However, students should address how they made their predictions. For example, a student may predict that a rock has an outside volume of 20 mL because it is shaped like a rectangular prism and it appears to be about one-fourth the volume of the Relational GeoSolids rectangular prism.

1b. Again, student answers will vary. For example, a student may measure the dimensions of the rock. If the height of the rock were 0.5 in., the width of the base were 1 in., and the length of the base were 2.25 in., then the volume of the rock would be:

(0.5 in.)(1 in.)(2.25 in.) = 1.125 in.^{3} or

(1.125 in.^{3})(16 mL/in.^{3}) = 18 mL.

1c. Answers will vary, but students should show evidence of using water displacement to determine volume, as they did in this activity. For example, a student may fill the beaker to 400 mL, immerse the rock in the water, and find that the water rises to a level of 425 mL. Therefore, the rock has an outside volume of 25 mL.

1d. Student answers will vary, but students should compare their estimates with the actual volumes they obtained via water displacement.

2a. The outside volume and inside volume determine the percentage of volume lost. These solids have about the same outside volume, but the rectangular prism has less inside volume because it has corners. The edges come together in the corners, making the plastic thicker there, decreasing the inside volume.

2b. Since the rectangular prism has more corners, and therefore more overlapping edges, the difference between the two volumes is greater for this prism. So, when you divide this higher number by the outside volume (80 mL), you get a higher percentage of volume lost for the rectangular prism than for the sphere.

Investigation 12: How Do Volume, Mass, and Density Relate?

Just because two objects have the same volume, they do not necessarily have the same mass. A baseball has a diameter similar to that of a tennis ball, yet the baseball weighs much more because it has greater density. Density is used in many applications. For example, chemists use density to determine concentrations of solutions, gemologists use it to tell similar gems apart, and auto mechanics use it to test battery acid and antifreeze. Density has applications in physics, engineering, geology, astronomy, biology, and many other fields.

Is it gold or just fool's gold?

Topic
of Investigation

Relationships among volume, mass, and density

Questions
to Investigate

▶ *How are mass, volume, and density related?*

▶ *How do you determine the density of a substance?*

▶ *What does the density of a substance tell you?*

Mathematical Review

Mass The measure of the amount of matter a substance contains. You will fill different Relational GeoSolids with various substances and then use a balance to determine their masses (in grams).

Volume The capacity of an object, i.e., how much an object holds, or how much space it takes up. The volume of an object may be expressed in cubic units, such as cm^3, or units of liquid volume, such as mL. You will fill the different solids with water to measure their capacities in mL.

Density The amount of matter per unit of space, usually reported as the amount of mass per unit of volume. Units for density, therefore, may be gm/cm^3, $lb/in.^3$, gm/mL, etc. To find the densities of the various substances, you will need the following formula:

$$\rho = m/V,$$

where ρ = density, m = mass, and V = volume.

Predict the Results

Without measuring, predict the relative densities of each of the substances listed in the Predictions Chart. Remember that density is the mass of a substance per unit of volume. Write your predictions in the chart below.

Predictions Chart: Which Substance Has the Greatest Density?

Substance	Ranking by Density (1 = greatest; 6 = least)
Salt	
Rice	
Water	
Isopropyl Alcohol	
Corn Syrup	
Vegetable Oil	

Procedure

1. Weigh each geometric solid listed in Results Chart 1 to the nearest gram. Record their masses in the first row.

2. Remove the circular stopper from the green base of the large cube. Using a funnel (if one is provided), carefully fill the cube with salt. Replace the stopper once the solid is completely filled. Weigh the filled cube to the nearest gram.

3. To find the mass of the substance, subtract the mass of the unfilled cube from the mass of the filled cube. Record the difference in the second row.

4. Repeat steps 2 and 3 for each solid and substance in the chart. Reuse the substances to fill the other solids. Use the substances in the order given, being sure to wipe out the solids between fillings. You will need to wash them out after using the corn syrup and vegetable oil.

5. Fill the solids with water again.

Materials

For each pair of students:

▶ *1 Relational Geosolids set*

▶ *A metric balance (with a mass set of 250 g)*

▶ *A graduated cylinder (marked in 2 mL increments)*

▶ *A funnel (optional), calculator, and paper towels*

▶ *$\frac{2}{3}$ cup each of salt, rice, water, isopropyl alcohol, corn syrup, and vegetable oil*

To determine the volume of each
solid to the nearest milliliter,
carefully pour the water from
each solid into a graduated cylinder.
Record each volume in Results Chart 2.

6. Calculate the density of each
substance by dividing the mass
of the substance by the volume.
Record your answers in Results Chart 2.

7. Find the mean density of each substance, ranking them according to their mean
densities. Record your results in Results Chart 2.

Hint

▶ *When filling the geometric solids with rice
and salt, occasionally tap the solids on the
table to settle the grains. Try to completely
fill all the corners with the liquids,
eliminating any large air bubbles.*

Results Chart 1: Masses of Substances [in gm]

Substance	Large Cube	Rectangular Prism	Square Prism	Small Cube	Square Pyramid
Unfilled solid					
Salt only					
Rice only					
Water only					
Isopropyl Alcohol only					
Corn Syrup only					
Vegetable Oil only					

Results Chart 2: Volumes of Solids and Densities of Substances

	Large Cube	Rectangular Prism	Square Prism	Small Cube	Square Pyramid		
Volume (in mL):							
Substance	Density (in gm/mL)					Mean Density	Ranking (1 = greatest; 6 = least)
Salt							
Rice							
Water							
Corn Syrup							
Vegetable Oil							

Discussion Questions

1. Compare your predictions with your results.

    a. Do your predictions match your results? If not, how are they different?

    b. Explain why your predictions differ from your results.

2. The four liquids you used in this activity can be poured into the same clear glass in such a way that they form four distinct layers. Review the densities of each of these liquids to determine which liquid would make up each of the layers below.

    a. Layer A _____

    b. Layer B _____

    c. Layer C _____

    d. Layer D _____

    Layer A

    Layer B

    Layer C

    Layer D

3. Rice grains generally sink in water, yet in this activity, the rice should have turned out to be less dense than water. Explain this apparent contradiction. Why does the rice appear to be less dense than the water in this activity?

4. Ice floats in water but sinks in isopropyl alcohol.

    a. Explain why this happens in terms of density.

    b. Would ice float or sink in corn syrup? Explain.

5. The ratio between the volume of the large cube and the volume of the square pyramid is approximately 3:1. Do your results for both mass and volume reflect this relationship? Explain your answer and include examples.

Further Investigations

1. If the masses of two Relational GeoSolids Large Cubes that are filled with two different substances differed by a few grams, what difference would you expect to see between two Small Cubes filled with the same substances? Explain.

2. If the masses of two Small Cubes that are filled with two different substances differed by a few grams, what difference would you expect to see between two Large Cubes filled with the same substances? Explain.

3. A prospector finds a 5 cm^3 nugget while panning for gold. The mass of this is about 100 grams. The density of gold is about 19 g/cm^3, while the density of fool's gold is only about 5 g/cm^3. Is this nugget more likely to be gold or fool's gold? Explain.

Objectives

- Determining the densities of different substances.

- Exploring how mass, volume, and density are related.

Getting Started Display two identical, clear glasses, one containing isopropyl alcohol; the other, water. Make sure the glasses are filled to the same level. Ask students whether the two liquids are the same and how they can tell without smelling or tasting the liquids. (Some students may suggest weighing them, thus indicating that they know something about density being a property of a substance. If they do suggest weighing the liquids, ask students to explain why this might be a useful method.) Ask students to define the term *density*. Explain that, in addition to weighing the liquids, you could compare their densities to the densities of another substance. To demonstrate, place one ice cube in each glass and point out that the ice floats in water, but sinks in alcohol. Ask students why ice behaves this way.

Explain that by comparing the densities of the two liquids to the density of ice, you can determine that they are different substances.

Ask whether the density of a substance is dependent upon temperature. They should understand from the different densities of water and ice that density is indeed dependent upon temperature.

Note: This activity will take longer than one class period. If time is a concern, we suggest breaking the work among groups. The simplest method to use is to assign each group to find the mass of all the substances in a particular solid and then to share their results with other groups.

Mathematical Review Go over the review provided on the student pages. Be sure that students understand each of the terms.

Predict the Results Remind students to make thoughtful predictions and not to change them as they work.

Procedure

1. Circulate among students to ensure that they understand the task. Ask them whether the solids are really empty. [*No, they contain air.*]

2. Make sure that students completely fill each solid, but that the circular stopper still fits snuggly in the green base.

3. Hint: Have students fill the solids over cafeteria trays to confine spills and make cleanup easier.

4. Have students take note that the units reflect mass per unit volume (i.e., g/mL); make sure that they use the correct masses (i.e., the net weights) to determine the densities.

5. If necessary, review how to determine the mean of data with the class.

Results Chart 1: Masses of Substances (in grams)

Substance	Large Cube	Rectangular Prism	Square Prism	Small Cube	Square Pyramid
Unfilled solid	36	22	15	9	20
Salt only	168	84	40	21	60
Rice only	106	52	25	13	37
Water only	122	60	30	16	43
Alcohol only	107	53	26	13	38
Corn syrup only	168	84	41	22	60
Vegetable oil only	112	56	27	14	40

How Do Volume, Mass, and Density Relate?

Results Chart 2: Volumes of Solids and Densities of Substances

	Large Cube	Rect. Prism	Square Prism	Small Cube	Square Pyramid		
Volume (in mL):	1.23	61	30	16	45		
Substance	Density (in gm/mL)					Mean Density	Ranking (1 = greatest; 6 = least)
Salt	1.37	1.38	1.33	1.31	1.33	1.34	2
Rice	0.86	0.85	0.83	0.81	0.82	0.83	6
Water	0.99	0.98	1.00	1.00	0.96	0.99	3
Alcohol	0.87	0.87	0.87	0.81	0.84	0.85	5
Corn syrup	1.37	1.38	1.37	1.37	1.33	1.36	1
Vegetable oil	0.91	0.92	0.90	0.88	0.89	0.90	4

Discussion Questions

1a. Predictions and answers will vary. Students should, however, address whether their predictions match their results and how they are different.

1b. Answers will vary. For example, a student may indicate that her predictions differ from her results because she thought that the rice would be more dense than the water, as rice usually sinks in water.

2a. Layer A—Isopropyl alcohol

2b. Layer B—Vegetable oil

2c. Layer C—Water

2d. Layer D—Corn syrup

3. The rice appears to be less dense than water in this activity because there is air between the grains when it is in a Relational GeoSolid.

4a. Ice is less dense than water, so it floats in water. Ice is denser than isopropyl alcohol, so it sinks in isopropyl alcohol.

4b. Ice would float in corn syrup, because ice is less dense than water, and water is less dense than corn syrup. Therefore, ice is less dense than corn syrup.

5. Answers will vary. Students should, however, compare their mass and volume results for the large cube and the square pyramid and tell whether their results show an approximate 3:1 ratio for volume and for masses of corresponding substances. Students should also give examples to support their answers.

Further Investigations

1. The difference between the masses of the filled small cubes should be less, because the volume of the small cube is $\frac{1}{8}$ the volume of the large cube. Thus, the difference between the masses of the filled small cubes should be about $\frac{1}{8}$ the difference between the masses of the filled large cubes.

2. The difference between the masses of the filled large cubes should be greater, because the volume of the large cube is 8 times the volume of the small cube. Thus, the difference between the masses of the filled large cubes should be about 8 times the difference between the masses of the filled small cubes.

3. The nugget is probably gold, not fool's gold. A 5 cm^3 nugget would weigh about 95 g, because 5 cm^3 × 19 g/cm^3 = 95 g, which is close to 100 g. A 5 cm^3 nugget of fool's gold, on the other hand, would only weigh about 25 g, because 5 cm^3 × 5 g/cm^3 = 25 g.

Investigation 13: Why Do Animals Curl Up When Cold?

Animals tend to curl up like a ball when they are cold because it helps them to keep warm. How? When an animal curls up, it changes its shape. This change decreases the rate at which the animal's body heat is lost. The animal is actually using geometry to solve a problem! In this activity you will investigate how changing the shape of an object affects its surface area. You will then relate this concept to real life problems and natural processes.

Topic of Investigation

Relationships among volume, shape, and surface area

Questions to Investigate

▶ *Do different-shaped solids with the same volume have the same surface area?*

▶ *How does the shape of an object affect its surface area?*

▶ *How does surface area affect chemical, biological, and physical processes?*

Mathematical Review

Surface area The sum of the areas of all the surfaces of a figure. For example, to find the surface area of a rectangular prism, first you need to find the area of each face, including the bases, then add them all together. Because some of the faces are congruent, you may take a shortcut and just find the area of one of each set of congruent faces, then multiply the result by the number of faces in that set.

Volume The capacity of a shape, i.e., how much the shape can hold, or how much space the shape takes up. The volumes of different types of solids are found using different formulas. For example, to find the volume of a rectangular prism, multiply the length, *l*, by the width, *w*, by the height, *h*.

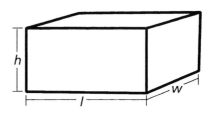

Investigating with Relational GeoSolids™

Predict the Results

For each type of Relational GeoSolid listed, predict the total number of each one that is needed for a total volume of 8 inches^3. Next, suppose you had that many of each type of solid, and you placed each set of identical geometric solids in a row, smallest end-to-smallest end, to form a new solid. You would now have three solids with the same volume. Will the surface areas of these new solids also be the same? Predict the relative size of the surface areas of the 3 new solids, with 1 being the greatest and 3 being the least. If you predict that the surface areas will be the same, give them the same number.

Predictions Chart: Surface Areas of Rectangular Prisms with Equal Volumes

Relational GeoSolids Shape	Number Needed for Volume to Equal 8 inches^3	Ranking by Surface Area of New Solid (1 = greatest 3 = least)	Reason for Ranking
Large Cube			
Square Prism			
Rectangular Prism			

Procedure

1. Measure the dimensions of the large cube, the square prism, and the rectangular prism to the nearest inch. Determine the volume of each of these geometric solids.

2. For each solid, determine how many would be needed for a total volume of 8 inches^3. Record your results in the Results Chart.

3. Suppose you had the number of each type of geometric solid needed for a total of 8 inches^3. If you placed each set of identical solids in a row, smallest end to smallest end, what would the dimensions of each new solid be? (See example.)

 Correct    Incorrect

4. Now, determine the total surface area of each new solid. Show your work and record your results in the Results Chart.

Results Chart: Surface Areas of Rectangular Prisms with Equal Volumes

Relational GeoSolids™ Shape	Number Needed for Volume to Equal 8 inches³	Dimensions and Total Surface Area of New Solid		Ranking by Surface Area of New Solid (1 = greatest 3 = least)
Large Cube		Dimensions:		
		Surface Area:		
Square Prism		Dimensions:		
		Surface Area:		
Rectangular Prism		Dimensions:		
		Surface Area:		

Discussion Questions

1. Compare your predictions with your results.

    a. Do your predictions match your results? If not, how are they different?

    b. Explain why your predictions differ from your results.

2. Look at the surface areas of the different solids formed.

    a. For solids with equal volumes, how does the surface area of a thinner or flatter solid compare to that of a thicker, more cubical solid?

    b. Which of these more closely resembles a ball: a long, flat, rectangular prism or a cube?

    c. The amount of available surface area affects the rates at which heat, gases, water, etc., can be exchanged with the surrounding environment. When it is cold, animals often curl up in the shape of ball to sleep, because it helps them to keep warm. Conversely, when it is hot, they often stretch themselves out when they sleep. Explain these behaviors in terms of surface area and heat exchange.

3. Suppose you have two bowls, each containing an equal amount of hot soup. One bowl has a larger diameter than the other one so the soup is much shallower in it. Which bowl of soup will cool off faster? Explain your answer in terms of surface area.

Investigating with Relational GeoSolids™

4. Jackrabbits and elephants live in hot climates. Both have large, thin ears. Explain how their ears help them to keep cool. Refer to surface area in your explanation.

5. If you wanted to build a box with a volume of 64 ft³ using the least amount of wood, what dimensions should your box have? Explain.

Further Investigations

1. Study and compare the shapes of cacti and their "leaves" to the shapes of tropical plants and their leaves.

    a. How do they differ?

    b. How does surface area relate to the adaptations ("survival tactics") of these plants?

2. All other factors being equal, which keep your hands warmer: mittens or gloves? Explain your thinking, referring to surface area in your explanation. (*Hint:* Trace around your hand with your fingers spread apart. Then trace around your hand with your four fingers together, but with your thumb sticking out. Think of your hand as a prism-type solid, and the two outlines of your hand being different-shaped bases.)

3. Flatworms, known as *planarians*, are very flat, fairly primitive, multicellular organisms. They live in moist areas and exchange gases, such as oxygen and carbon dioxide, directly through their body surfaces. How is "flatness" advantageous to these organisms? Explain your answer in terms of surface area.

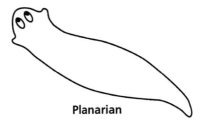
Planarian

4. Naturally formed objects tend to conserve resources. Why are bubbles naturally spherical instead of cubical? Explain your thinking and refer to surface area in your explanation. (*Hint:* Determine and compare the surface areas of a cube and a sphere that have the same volume.)

Objectives

- Explore how changes in shape affect surface area.

- Relate surface area and volume to biological, chemical, and physical processes.

Getting Started Form a fist-sized ball out of modeling clay. Direct students' attention as you smash the ball into a pancake shape. Ask students whether you have changed the volume of the object. Encourage students to discuss their answers, then explain to them that, in fact, the volume of the clay was not affected. Ask them whether you have changed the surface area of the object. Solicit student responses, but do not give students any definitive answers. Instead, tell students that, in

this activity, they will investigate whether changing the shape of an object, but not its volume, affects its surface area. Explain to students that they will explore this question through the "virtual construction" of different shaped, rectangular prisms with equal volumes. They will then relate this concept to real life and natural processes.

Mathematical Review Go over the review provided on the student pages. Be sure that students understand each of the terms and how to find the surface area and volume of a rectangular prism.

Predict the Results Remind students to make thoughtful predictions and not to change their predictions as they work.

Procedure

1. Although students may want to record the dimensions and volumes of the Relational GeoSolids somewhere as they work, these are not the dimensions referred to in the Results Chart.

2. Circulate among students to ensure that they understand the task. You may want to allow students to borrow Geosolids from other groups in order to create the correct new solids.

3. Remind students to consider the exposed edges only when determining the dimensions of each new solid.

4. Remind students to consider the exposed faces only when determining the total surface area of each new solid.

Results Chart: Surface Areas of Rectangular Prisms with Equal Volumes

Relational GeoSolids™ Shape	Number Needed for Volume to Equal 8 inches^3	Dimensions and Total Surface Area of New Solid	Ranking by Surface Area of New Solid 1 = greatest 3 = least
Large Cube	1	dimensions: 2" × 2" × 2" surface area: 6(4 inches^2) = 24 inches^2	3
Square Prism	4	dimensions: 1" × 1" × 8" surface area: 2(1 inches^2) + 4(8 inches^2) = 34 inches^2	1
Rectangular Prism	2	dimensions: 4" × 1" × 2" surface area: 2(2 in.^{2}) + 2(4 in.^{2}) + 2(8 in.^{2}) = 28 in.^{2}	2

Discussion Questions

1a. Predictions and answers will vary. Students should, however, address whether their predictions match their results, and how they are different.

1b. Answers will vary. For example, a student may indicate that his predictions differ from his results because he thought that objects with the same volume would have the same surface area.

2a. The thinner or flatter solid has a greater surface area.

2b. A cube more closely resembles a ball.

2c. A ball shape has relatively less surface area than a stretched-out shape. So, a ball shape decreases heat loss, and a stretched-out shape increases heat loss.

3. The shallow bowl of soup would cool down faster, because more of the soup is exposed to the air, so the heat can escape more easily. The shallow bowl of soup has more surface area exposed.

4. The large, thin ears of jackrabbits and elephants help them keep cool because they have a lot of surface area and very little volume, so the heat can easily escape from the animal.

5. A 4 ft × 4 ft × 4 ft box would require the least amount of wood, because the more cubical a shape is, the less surface area it has.

Further Investigations

1a. Cacti are generally thicker and rounder than tropical plants (not including trees), and their leaves are reduced to small, dry spines. The leaves of tropical plants, on the other hand, are usually large, very flat, and broad.

1b. The thicker, rounder shapes of cacti mean that they have less surface area than do thinner plants of equal volumes. This reduced surface area decreases water loss from the plant, which helps cacti live in the desert. The broad, flat shapes of the tropical leaves increases the surface area for photosynthesis and for secreting excess water, if necessary.

2. Mittens keep your hands warmer than gloves. Because the fingers are together in a mitten, there is less surface area of the mitten in contact with the cold air. Thus, there is less surface area through which body heat can escape.

3. The planarian's flat shape means it has a lot of surface area per unit of volume. Thus, there is more surface area for gas exchange to occur.

4. Answers will vary, but students should adequately support their answers with an example, such as:

"A cube with a volume of 1 inch^3 has a surface area of 6 inches^2, $(6(1")^2) = 6$ inches^2).

"A sphere with a volume of 1 inch^3 has a surface of about 4.8 inches^2, (1 inch$^3 = \frac{4}{3}\pi r^3$, so $r = 0.62$ inch; $4\pi(0.62")^2 = 4.8$ inches^2).

"Thus, a sphere has less surface area than a cube of equal volume, which means that less material is needed to form the surface of the sphere than the surface of the cube."

Investigation 14: Why Do Elephants Wear Mud Hats?

When it gets very hot, elephants pack mud on their heads. Why? Since the temperature of the mud is lower than that of the air, the wet mud cools the elephant off, just like bathing in a waterhole does. Additionally, the mud helps to insulate the elephant's head from the sun's heat, like a hat does for a human. Why does an elephant need this extra means of staying cool? The answer is in the elephant's large size and round shape—in other words, its high volume and relatively low surface area. In this investigation, you will determine how the size of an object or organism affects surface area and volume. You will then compare objects of different sizes and shapes by their surface area-to-volume ratios and finally relate what you discover to real-life problems.

Topic of Investigation

Surface area-to-volume ratios

Questions to Investigate

▶ *How does surface area relate to volume?*

▶ *How does the size of an object affect its surface area?*

▶ *How does the surface area-to-volume ratio of an object affect biological, chemical, and physical processes?*

Mathematical Review

Surface Area The sum of the areas of all the surfaces of a figure. For example, to find the surface area of a rectangular prism, you need to find the area of each face, including the bases, then add them all together. Because some of the faces are congruent, you may take a shortcut and just find the area of one of each set of congruent faces and then multiply the result by the number of faces in that set.

Volume The capacity of a shape, i.e., how much the shape can hold, or how much space the shape takes up. The volumes of different types of solids are found using different formulas. To find the volume of a rectangular prism, for example, simply multiply the length, *l*, by the width, *w*, by the height, *h*.

Ratios The relation between two quantities, expressing the comparison in lowest terms. Fractions are one way of expressing ratios, but they may also be expressed using a colon. For example, if there are 15 girls and 10 boys in your class, there are 3 girls for every 2 boys. The ratio of the girls to the boys is written as 3:2. After you determine the surface area and volumes of the solids, you will determine the **surface area-to-volume ratio** for each. These ratios should be presented as a whole number to a whole number, in lowest terms.

Investigating with Relational GeoSolids™

Predict the Results

Without doing any calculations, predict how the surface area-to-volume ratios for each pair of geometric solids below will compare. For each pair, tell which will have the larger surface area-to-volume ratio. Explain your choices.

Predictions Chart: Comparing Surface Area-to-Volume Ratios of Different Sized Solids

Relational GeoSolids Shape	Which will have the greater surface area-to-volume ratio?	Explanation
Large Cube		
Small Cube		
Large Cylinder		
Small Cylinder		

Procedure

1. Measure the dimensions of each of the solids listed in the Results Chart to the nearest inch. Record your results in the first column of the Results Chart.

2. Determine the total surface area and volume of each solid. Show your work and list your answers in the second and third columns of the Results Chart.

3. Determine the surface area-to-volume ratio for each solid. Record your answers, in lowest terms, in the fourth column of the Results Chart.

4. Compare the surface area-to-volume ratios for each pair of solids. Record your answers in the fifth column of the Results Chart.

Materials

For each pair of students:

▶ *1 Relational GeoSolids set*

▶ *1 customary ruler*

▶ *1 calculator (optional)*

Hint

▶ *You should not need to convert your reduced ratios to compare them. They should all be in the form n:1, where n is a whole number.*

Results Chart: Surface Areas, Volumes, and Surface Area-to-Volume Ratios

Relational GeoSolids Shape	Dimensions (inches)	Total Surface Area (inches^2)	Volume (inches^3)	Surface Area-to-Volume Ratio (SA:V)	Which Has a Greater Surface Area-to-Volume Ratio?
Large Cube					
Small Cube					
Large Cylinder					
Small Cylinder					

Discussion Questions

1. Compare your predictions with your results.

    a. Do your predictions match your results? If not, how are they different?

    b. Explain why your predictions differ from your results.

2. Look at the data for the small and large cubes. Although each side of the large cube is twice as long as that of the small cube, the surface area and volume did not just increase by a factor of two.

    a. How many times greater is the surface area of the large cube than that of the small cube?

    b. How many times greater is the volume of the large cube than that of the small cube?

    c. Write the formulas for finding the surface area and the volume of a cube. Use the formulas to explain why the surface areas and volumes do not increase by the same factor when the dimensions are doubled.

3. If the length of each side of the smaller cube were tripled, how would each of the following change? Explain each answer.

    a. surface area

    b. volume

    c. surface area-to-volume ratio

88

Investigating with Relational GeoSolids™

4. Look at the data for the small and large cylinders. Note that only the diameter was doubled, not the height, but the surface areas and volumes do not increase proportionally.

   a. About how many times greater is the surface area of the large cylinder compared to the small cylinder?

   b. About how many times greater is the volume of the large cylinder compared to the small cylinder?

   c. Do the surface areas and volumes of the small cylinders increase by the same proportion when its diameter is doubled? Explain your answer; be sure to include how the surface area-to-volume ratios can be used to answer this question.

5. Now, think about heat loss in elephants, mice, and other *endothermic* (warm-blooded) animals. Endothermic animals maintain a constant body temperature by producing their own heat. Their bodies produce heat by breaking down sugar, starch, and fat molecules, which releases stored energy. Consider how the size difference between elephants and mice affects the rates at which they lose body heat.

   a. Explain how an elephant's large size makes it more difficult for it to lose excess heat compared to a mouse.

   b. Despite their small size, mice, hummingbirds, and other tiny, endothermic animals need to eat frequently. Explain why this is so, in terms of their size and surface area-to-volume ratios.

Further Investigations

1. All other factors being equal, which would melt faster: crushed ice or an equal volume of block ice? Explain your answer in terms of surface area-to-volume ratio.

2. Why do blood vessels such as *villi* in your intestines and *alveoli* in your lungs branch into increasingly smaller units? Research the functions of these structures, and explain in terms of surface area-to-volume ratio how such "branching" is beneficial to us.

3. Why are enormous cells, such as the giant amoeba-type organism in the movie *The Blob* impossible in real life? That is, why are cells limited in size? Explain your answer in terms of surface area-to-volume ratio.

Investigating with Relational GeoSolids™

Objectives

- Explore how changes in size affect surface area, volume, and surface area-to-volume ratios.

- Relate size and surface area-to-volume ratios to biological, chemical, and physical processes.

Getting Started
Ask students whether an antacid tablet would dissolve faster in water when it is whole, or when it is crushed. Discuss with students that the crushed tablet should dissolve faster as long as the temperature of the water is the same in both cases. Ask students why this is so. Lead them to focus on the amount of surface area exposed to the water in each case. (Consider presenting this as either a demonstration or a hands-on investigation for students.) Explain that even though the volume of the antacid is the same, the rate of dissolution is slower for the tablet because it has less surface area exposed to the water. Therefore, the antacid's surface area-to-volume ratio affects the rate at which it dissolves.

Tell students that they will be exploring how size affects surface area, volume, and surface area-to-volume ratio. They will then relate these concepts to real life processes.

Mathematical Review
Go over the review on the student pages. Be sure students understand each of the terms. Consider working a sample problem such as the following with the class:

> Compare the surface area-to-volume ratios of a 4" cube to a 2" × 3" × 4" rectangular prism.
>
> [The SA:V of the cube = 3:2 and the SA:V of the rectangular prism = 13:6, so the SA:V ratio of the rectangular prism is greater.]

Predict the Results
Remind students to make thoughtful predictions and not to change them as they work.

Procedure

1. Circulate among students to ensure that they understand the task and that they round the measurements to the nearest inch.

2. Remind students to include both bases when they calculate the total surface area of the solids. Also, suggest to students that they leave the surface areas and volumes of the cylinders in terms of π to make it easier to determine their surface area-to-volume ratios.

3. Remind students to express the ratios in whole numbers and lowest terms and to present the ratios in the correct order.

4. Remind students to clearly state which solid is larger in each pair.

Results Chart: Surface Areas, Volumes, and Surface Area-to-Volume Ratios

Relational GeoSolids™ Shape	Dimensions (inches)	Total Surface Area (inches²)	Volume (inches³)	Surface Area-to-Volume Ratio (SA:V)	Which has a greater surface area-to-volume ratio?
Large Cube	2" × 2" × 2"	$6(4 \text{ inches}^2) = 24 \text{ inches}^2$	$(2")^3 = 8 \text{ inches}^3$	3:1	The small cube
Small Cube	1" × 1" × 1"	$6(1 \text{ inch}^2) = 6 \text{ inches}^2$	$(1")^3 = 1 \text{ inches}^3$	6:1	The small cube
Large Cylinder	radius = 1" height = 2"	$2\pi(1")(2") + 2\pi(1")^2 = 6\pi \text{ inches}^2$	$\pi(1")^2(2") = 2\pi \text{ inches}^3$	3:1	The small cylinder
Small Cylinder	radius = 0.5" height = 2"	$2\pi(0.5")(2") + 2\pi(0.5")^2 = 2.5\pi \text{ inches}^2$	$\pi(0.5")^2(2") = 0.5\pi \text{ inches}^3$	5:1	The small cylinder

Why Do Elephants Wear Mud Hats?

Discussion Questions

1a. Predictions and answers will vary. Students should, however, address whether their predictions match their results, and how they are different.

1b. Answers will vary. For example, a student may indicate that his predictions differ from his results because he did not really think about the problem in terms of ratios. He may indicate that he assumed the ratio would be larger for the larger solids, simply because the surface areas and volumes would be larger.

2a. The surface area of the large cube is 4 times greater than that of the small cube.

2b. The volume of the large cube is 8 times greater than that of the small cube.

2c. The formula for the surface area of a cube is $6s^2$. The formula for the volume of a cube is s^3. The surface area and volume of a cube do not increase by the same amount when the dimensions of the cube are doubled, because volume increases by a power of 3, whereas surface area only increases by a power of 2. Thus, volume increases by a factor of 8 ($2^3 = 8$) and surface area increases by a factor of 4 ($2^2 = 4$).

3a. The surface area of the cube would be 9 times that of the small cube, because the surface area would increase by 3^2.

3b. The volume of the large cube would be 27 times that of the small cube, because the volume would increase by 3^3.

3c. The surface area-to-volume ratio would decrease from 6:1 to 2:1, because the surface area would equal 54 inches^2, $6(3")^2 = 54$ inches^2, and the volume would equal 27 inches^3, $(3")^3 = 27$ inches^3

4a. The surface area increased by a little more than a factor of 2 (by 2.4 times).

4b. The volume increased by a factor of 4.

4c. No, the surface areas and volumes did *not* increase proportionally. If they had, the surface area-to-volume ratios would be the same, and they are not. The surface area-to-volume ratio decreased from 5:1 to 3:1.

5a. An elephant has a small surface area compared to its volume because it is very large (and very round). Surface area-to-volume ratio decreases as size increases, unless the object organism changes its basic body shape (i.e., becomes much thinner or has many thin, branching appendages).

5b. Small animals tend to lose heat rapidly because they have large surface area-to-volume ratios. Thus, they need to eat frequently so they have a constant supply of energy to keep themselves warm.

Further Investigations

1. Crushed ice will melt faster, because the smaller pieces provide more surface area for heat exchange (absorption) to occur. The smaller pieces have larger surface area-to-volume ratios.

2. *Villi* are the intestinal structures where blood vessels meet so that nutrients and water can pass into the bloodstream. *Alveoli* are the lung structures where the blood vessels in the lungs meet to exchange carbon dioxide and oxygen. The sequential branching of these structures into increasingly smaller units increases the surface area available for these essential exchanges to occur. The smaller branches have larger surface area-to-volume ratios.

3. Cells are limited in size due to the constraints of surface area-to-volume ratios. As they increase in size, the amount of surface area relative to the amount of volume decreases. Cells exchange water, gases, nutrients, and other chemicals through their cell membranes. As the volume increases, the demands for such essential substances increases, but the relative amount of surface area (cell membrane) available for exchanging substances decreases. Thus, the efficiency of this simple method of transporting substances in and out of a cell becomes inadequate when cells become too large.

apex the corner of a pyramid opposite the base at which all vertical faces meet

base the bottom face (and top if there is one) of a geometric solid; for Relational GeoSolids™ it is the green face

concave polygon a polygon in which at least two points can be connected by a line segment which is at least partially outside of the polygon

convex polygon a polygon in which any two points can be connected by a line segment which lies entirely inside the polygon

cross section a shape formed by the intersection of a plane and a geometric solid

density the amount of matter a substance contains, determined by dividing the mass by the volume

edge the line segments formed where faces of a geometric solid intersect

face the planar (flat) surfaces of a geometric solid

geometric solid a three dimensional object, including spheres, cylinders, cones, prisms, and pyramids

intersecting lines lines which have exactly one point in common

intersecting planes planes which have exactly one line in common

lateral area the area of the surfaces, excluding the bases, of a geometric solid

net a two-dimensional pattern which can be folded to form a three-dimensional solid

parallel lines lines which are in the same plane but have no point in common

parallel planes planes which do not have a line of intersection

perpendicular lines two lines that intersect at right angles

plane a flat surface that extends infinitely and has no thickness

polygon a closed two-dimensional shape consisting of three or more straight sides

prism a geometric solid consisting of rectangles connecting two congruent, parallel polygon bases

pyramid a geometric solid consisting of a polygon base and triangular sides meeting at a common vertex

ratio a mathematical statement expressing how two or more values compare

skew lines lines which are not in the same plane and therefore are neither parallel nor intersecting

surface area the total area of all surfaces, sides and base(s), of a geometric solid

vertex a corner, or where three or more faces come together

volume the capacity of an object, either the amount of space an object takes up or the amount of space inside the object

Assessment Chart

Scoring Rubric

4 Exemplary   Student's reply is consistent with correct mathematical concepts. Student clearly communicates understanding of the important mathematical concepts, ideas, and processes. Response includes well-organized justification, pictures, charts, or diagrams.

3 Substantial   Student shows essential understanding of the mathematical concepts involved. Written work provided is partially correct. Student may have made minor computational errors or errors in reasoning.

2 Partial   Student exhibits partial understanding of the mathematical concepts. Written work is provided but is incomplete or unclear.

1 Insufficient   Student shows little understanding of the mathematical concepts. Explanations provided are unclear with no support or justification.

Student Name	Investigation														Total of 56 Rubric points	Comments
	1	2	3	4	5	6	7	8	9	10	11	12	13	14		

Relational GeoSolids™ Template

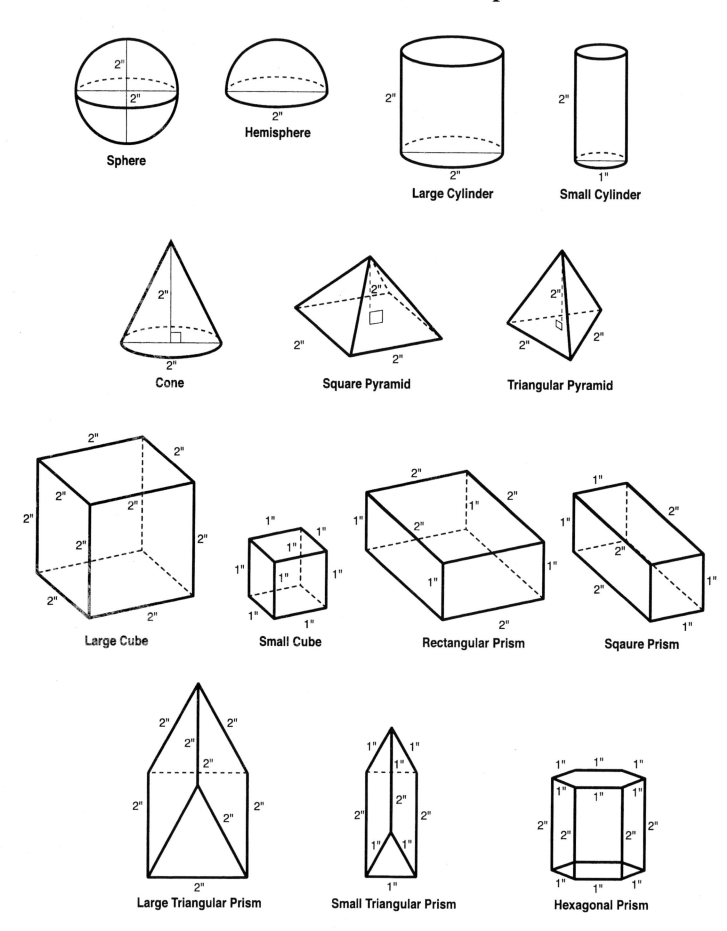

Sphere

Hemisphere

Large Cylinder

Small Cylinder

Cone

Square Pyramid

Triangular Pyramid

Large Cube

Small Cube

Rectangular Prism

Sqaure Prism

Large Triangular Prism

Small Triangular Prism

Hexagonal Prism